The Third Commandment
and the Return of the Anusim:

A Rabbi's Memoir of an Incredible People

Photo Don Scharf

Rabbi Stephen Leon

The Third Commandment
and the Return of the Anusim:

A Rabbi's Memoir of an Incredible People

Gaon Books
www.gaonbooks.com

For permissions, group pricing, and other information contact Gaon Books, P.O. Box 23924, Santa Fe, NM 87502 or write (gaonbooks@gmail.com).

Manufactured in the United States of America.

The paper used in this publication is acid free and meets all ANSI (American National Standards for Information Sciences) standards for archival quality paper. All wood product components used in this book are Sustainable Forest Initiative (SFI) certified.

Library of Congress Cataloging-in-Publication Data

Names: Leon, Stephen, 1945- author.
Title: The Third commandment and the return of the Anusim : a rabbi's memoir of an incredible people / Rabbi Stephen Leon.
Description: [Santa Fee, New Mexico] : Gaon Books, [2017]
Identifiers: LCCN 2017023207 | ISBN 9781935604082 (pbk. : alk. paper)
Subjects: LCSH: Jews--Texas--El Paso. | Crypto-Jews--Texas--El Paso--cultural assimilation. | Leon, Stephen, 1945- | Rabbis--Texas--El Paso--Biography. | El Paso (Tex.)--Ethnic relations.
Classification: LCC F394.E4 L46 2017 | DDC 305.892/4076496--dc23

LC record available at https://lccn.loc.gov/2017023207

Cover and Frontispiece photos courtesy of Don Scharf

Table of Contents

I dedicate this work to my beautiful wife, Sharon, who has been at my side and encouraged me for almost half a century. I pray that my three grandchildren, Daniel, Jordyn, and Emme, who have given me so much love, will one day see a world of peace for their generation.

Foreword

RABBI STEPHEN LEON'S BOOK, *THE THIRD COM-mandment and the Return of the Anusim: a Rabbi's Memoir of an Incredible People*, stands as not only a testimony of faith, but also as a symbol of religious tenacity.

Anusim is the Hebrew word first employed by fif-teenth century Spanish Jews to describe their co-reli-gionists who were forced either by the sword or other means to convert to Christianity. These people were often called by many other names, some complimentary and others carrying a disparaging nuance. These names in-cluded *marranos, conversos,* and *nuevos cristianos.* Jews, however, used but one word: *anusim*: meaning those who had been spiritually violated.

Fifteenth and sixteenth century Spanish Jews saw these people as the victims of a spiritual assault. Although it is true that some of these people, once converted, did become loyal citizens of Christendom, others, despite the trials and tribulations maintained a schizophrenic split religious personality. That is to say, that on the outside these anusim by law were practicing Christians, but in the interiors of their homes and souls, they remained loy-al to the faith and people of Israel.

These forced conversions changed the social struc-ture of Spanish Jewry. Where once there had been a sin-gle and united Jewish politic within the various nations that composed the Iberian Peninsula, now Jewry was divided into four separate subcategories:

(1) Jews who were practicing members of the people of Israel,

(2) Jews had converted to Christianity due to issues of spiritual assault but despite the legal and economic hurdles remained at least in private loyal to their faith and people,

10

(3) Jews, who were forced to convert, decided to adapt themselves to their new situation and became loyal Catholics and

(4) a small number of Jews who for personal reasons had freely chosen Christianity.

The above situation created consequences, not only for the wounded Jewish community, but also for Spanish society as a whole. Once converted, Christian doctrine argued that there was no return and that the anusim were to be considered full Christians. This policy meant that converted Jews, although separated from the Jewish community, no longer suffered from anti-Semitic laws. The unintended consequences of this policy resulted in converted Jews rising quickly into the ranks of all branches of Spanish society and provoking a backlash and a great amount of anxiety among the "old Christians." It is out of this backlash and hostility that the Inquisition was established. Its job? To root out heresy among those who had *sangre sucia* (dirty blood).

It should be emphasized that the Inquisitors could not touch Jews who had never converted. In 1492 the King and Queen of Spain, Ferdinand and Isabella, put an end to thousands of years of Iberian Jewish history, declaring Spain to be *Judenrein,* and giving Spanish Jews the choice of immigration (expulsion) or conversion. After 1492 Judaism was illegal in Spain and would remain so for the next five centuries until the final reconciliation and official degree of apology promulgated in Madrid in 1992. For those anusim now caught in the Inquisition's clutches it was their blood rather than their faith that would determine their ultimate fate. For many of these people their only hope was emigration to the far distant corners of the Spanish empire.

During these five centuries, many of the most loyal anusim were able to flee Spain and made their way to New Spain, parts of which now compose the southwestern United States. In New Spain, anusim continued to live a religiously schizophrenic existence. Out of necessity, American anusim created new cultural patterns. They created this new "society within a society" as means of hiding their "other identity" from the Church, government officials, and even the prying of nosy neighbors. Many of these people knew little about their family histories, and often believed that certain family customs were simply quaint quirks or unique family customs.

The distinguished New Mexican scholar Stanley Hordes is perhaps the first professional historian to help the anusim realize that they were a distinct ethnic group within Latino culture. Since Hordes pioneering works, more Latinos began to explore if and how they were connected to the lost world of the anusim. This small sociological stream slowly turned into a river as hundreds and perhaps thousands of Latinos now seek to learn about, and for some recapture, a lost part of their cultural, religious, and social heritage. Additionally the modern techniques associated with DNA testing have opened numerous portals into personal ancestries.

Many of these potential anusim have sought out Rabbi Stephen Leon of El Paso. Although not himself a Latino by birth, Rabbi Leon quickly grasped that these were people, who were not merely seeking their past, but for many they were also seeking a spiritual home.

12   Having heard dozens and perhaps hundreds of personal stories, Rabbi Leon has collected them and here shares the joys and fears, the loves and anger of people, who only now are recuperating what was once taken from their forefathers and foremothers.

Their return to the Jewish people is more than a marriage of history to sociology; it is a renaissance of joy that gladdens the heart. These tales tell a story 500 years in the making. Statistically the probabilities of this book existing over 500 years after the event are almost nil, but Jewish history is not comprised merely of facts and numbers, it is the history of a people that refused to sink into history, the story of a people that simply refused to die. The stories told to us by Rabbi Leon are their stories, the stories of the Jewish nation and the story of each of us who seeks to live life in freedom and dignity.

Rabbi Peter Tarlow
Director for the Center of Latino-Jewish Relations
Houston, Texas

Introduction

THE STORY OF CRYPTO-JEWS, WHICH MEANS "hidden Jews", and their descendants, the B'nei Anusim, is probably the biggest secret in the world and in the Jewish community today. There are many reasons why I feel driven to write a book about what I believe to be the most important issue concerning the Jewish people. It is my hope and prayer that with the help of God the return of all the Jews, who were forcibly converted by the Catholic Church during the Spanish Inquisition, will become a reality in my lifetime. It has begun, and the signs of its potential are on the horizon.

When I read the third of the Ten Commandments, I cannot help but believe that God specifically designated this commandment for the crypto-Jews. The motivation behind my decision to put into writing the many experiences that I have shared with the B'nei Anusim (Children of the Forced Ones) is because I'm deeply touched by their story, and I'm passionate about bringing them back, as they return to Judaism.

I dedicate this book to some of the heroes of the crypto-Judaic story. They include Rabbi Nissan ben Avraham, Rabbi Juan Mejia, Dr. Stanley Hordes, Sonya Loya, Genie Milgrom, Rabbi Peter Tarlow, and hundreds of the crypto-Jews who have touched my life in so many ways.

I am grateful to Ron Duncan Hart, who inspired and guided me to finally complete this book, which I had started many times.

— Stephen Leon

Part One

The Anusim and their Stories

Chapter One

How And Why The B'nei Anusim
Are Returning Today

THE RETURN OF THE CRYPTO-JEWS HAS BECOME a personal story for me. I was born in Brooklyn, New York, raised in Bridgeport, Connecticut, and served as rabbi of the Elmwood Park Jewish Center in New Jersey from 1971-1986. During those first forty-one years of my life I never met a crypto-Jew. I had read about crypto-Jews and the Spanish Inquisition, but to me their story was just a small part of Jewish history. Then, something happened that changed my life forever.

In August of 1986 I became the rabbi of Congregation B'nai Zion, in El Paso, Texas. I was in my office just a few days when I received a phone call from a gentleman from Juarez, Mexico, which is just across the border from El Paso. The man asked if he could come and see me and called me, *Rabino*. I didn't even know that *rabino* was Spanish for rabbi. I agreed to meet with him the following day. The man came into my office and introduced himself. His first name was Jesus, but referred to himself as Chuyee. He told me that he was a practicing Catholic from Juarez who went to church every Sunday with his family and that his grandmother had passed away two weeks ago.

He continued by telling me that ever since he was a small child of three his grandmother would take him into a dark corner of the house on Friday evening and light two candles and say some words that he didn't understand. He was the only family member invited to watch this custom. Since his grandmother had died he assumed that his mother would carry on the practice, but she told her son that it was grandma's tradition, and she was not at all interested.

Chuyee was upset and asked other family members why this custom was no longer being practiced. Since he would not let up with his nagging, he was urged to speak to his priest. He told me that the priest answered him as follows, "There are hundreds of Catholic women lighting candles on Friday night in Juarez, and I know the reason why, but you should really ask a rabbi. He is the correct person to answer your question." That was his story, as he sat in front of me.

As I thought of how I would respond to his question, I couldn't stop thinking about the priest's words: "there are hundreds of Catholic women lighting candles on Friday night." I told the man that lighting candles on Friday night was a Jewish custom, and that Jewish women have been performing this tradition for centuries. His mouth dropped when he learned that this was a "Jewish" custom. That idea had never entered his mind. He asked further questions regarding the reasons why a religious Catholic woman like his grandmother would be performing a Jewish tradition and why his mother would refuse to continue the practice.

I responded that perhaps his grandmother was continuing a tradition of her grandmother before her and that possibly this was an indication that her family had Jewish ancestry dating back to the Spanish Inquisition when Jews began to practice such customs in secret. I suggested that since his mother did not identify with the Jewish ancestry, she did not think it was right to keep the practice alive. The man asked me if I would permit him to come to synagogue services, and I told him that whenever he wanted to, he was certainly welcome.

Three decades after I met him, I still see Chuyee at services, especially on the High Holy Days. He maintains his Catholic religion, but continues to be interested in his Jewish roots. That incident was just the beginning.

17

A few days later, I received a call from a woman in El Paso. Mrs. Gonzalez came to see me and told me that she was a practicing Catholic and that her aunt had just died. After the funeral in the Catholic tradition, everyone returned to the house of mourning. To her surprise, she noticed that the immediate family was sitting on low benches, that the mirrors were covered, and that some people had a tear in their garments.

When she asked why these traditions were being practiced, which she had never seen before, she was told that these were Jewish traditions. When she asked about the meaning of the traditions, no one knew. Finally, when Mrs. Gonzalez asked why there would be Jewish traditions practiced after a Catholic funeral service, she was told that her aunt had some Jewish ancestry. She was further confused because this meant that her own mother, the deceased aunt's sister, also would be of Jewish descent. She was shocked that her own mother never told her of the Jewish ancestry of the family.

I gave Mrs. Gonzalez an explanation for the various Jewish traditions that she had witnessed, and I surmised that once again there was a possibility that her aunt had been a descendant of Spanish Jews and had been practicing these Jewish traditions in secret.

After observing these two incidents within a few days of my moving to El Paso, I began to wonder if this was simply a coincidence or if perhaps there were remnants of crypto-Judaism here in the Southwest. It has often been said that "circumstances happen in threes", and sure enough, the very next day the third situation confronted me.

This time I was at home waiting for cable to be installed in my house. When the man arrived, he noticed a sign on my wall that read, "Shalom Y'all", which was a gift from congregants in my previous synagogue in New Jersey when we moved to El Paso. When the cable man, whose name was Jorge, saw the sign, he asked if I were Jewish. I told him that not only was I a Jew, but that I was a rabbi. As soon as he heard those words, he told me with a big smile that he was Jewish, too, and opened his shirt revealing a large Jewish Star.

I asked him where he attended synagogue, and he told me that he had not attended services, yet, for he had just learned that he was Jewish a few weeks ago. He proceeded to tell me that just before his grandmother had died, she called him into her bedroom and revealed to him that she was Jewish and so was he, and then handed him this Magen David, the Jewish Star, which had been in the family for generations. We talked more about Judaism as he was installing the cable.

When he left, I began to personally review these three incidents that I had experienced within my first week in

El Paso. There were a number of similarities. In each case the person who spoke to me did not know originally that they had Jewish ancestry until a death had taken place in the family. Secondly, the traditions, the lighting of candles, the covering of mirrors, or the Star of David, were clearly Jewish customs and may well have been part of that Catholic family for generations.

I began to do research on the phenomenon of B'nei Anusim and crypto-Jews in El Paso, Texas. The Reform congregation of El Paso is Temple Mt. Sinai and the rabbi at the time that I came to the community was Rabbi Kenneth Weiss, of blessed memory, who became a good friend over the years. I asked Ken about the crypto-Jews, and he said that he had not had experience with them, but suggested that I speak to the retired rabbi, Floyd Fierman, who had written books about the early history of the Jewish community of El Paso.

I read Rabbi Fierman's book, entitled, *Boots and Roots*, but I did not find any substantive information about crypto-Jews. I spoke to Floyd personally about the conversos, and discovered that he, too, had not been involved with them. I began to question myself and why people with crypto-Jewish backgrounds were beginning to come to me. Although my grandparents came from Eastern Europe, namely from Poland and Austria, my father and I had begun to do research into the my family name "Leon" and the Sephardic roots of our ancestry, which clearly came from Spain.

Even though I did not know of any family member of mine who died during the Holocaust, I learned that there were many with the name "Leon" who were expelled from Spain during the Inquisition. In fact, my own grandfather's Hebrew name was Moshe Leon, and he once told me that Moshe Leon was a common name in past generations in his family, suggesting that we might have genealogical ties to the great rabbi from thirteenth century Spain, Moshe de Leon, the author of the *Zohar*, the book of Kabbalah. Perhaps this is one of the reasons that crypto-Jews were beginning to find me in El Paso.

20

Since that first week that I came to the Southwest until today I have become passionate about the return of the crypto-Jews to Judaism. Let me share with you more of these experiences. About a month later, I was invited to a Friday evening service in Juarez, Mexico where I was told that a number of Jews would gather to worship on Shabbat periodically. They had a lay leader and wanted the new rabbi to come and visit with them.

When I came to the home where the service was held, I met about twenty-five families. Among the group I found some who were Jewish their entire lives, some intermarried couples, some who were exploring Judaism, some who were Messianic, some who had converted to Judaism, some who were in the process of converting, and some who were crypto-Jews who were deciding what to do with their background. To my knowledge three decades later, all but one of those families have moved to El Paso and have become part of my congregation. Some completed their conversion and some didn't. A number of them did study with me and made formal conversion or "return" to Judaism. Once again, being exposed to this interesting

Jewish community, and the fact that I was able to have an impact on them, was for me a part of the journey that had begun when I came to El Paso.

I have been involved in interfaith programs and services ever since I entered the rabbinate. I believe that by participating with other faith groups in study sessions, in seminars, pulpit exchanges, charitable causes, and religious services, we can break down the barriers that cause prejudice and misunderstanding and create a community of mutual understanding and unity.

A few years after becoming involved in interfaith activities in El Paso, I received a phone call from a woman Presbyterian minister with whom I had worked in interfaith programming. She said that she needed to talk with me as soon as possible. To hide her identity, I will call her Theresa. She came into my office, took a seat and immediately began to cry hysterically. I was taken by surprise, gave her a box of tissues, and kept trying to console her but to no avail.

After about six or seven minutes, Theresa said to me, "Rabbi, I need to ask you to grant me two favors, first to forgive me, and second, to give me permission to attend your synagogue on Yom Kippur, the Day of Atonement. Without giving me a chance to answer, Theresa began to tell me her story, "Rabbi Leon, my whole life has been dedicated to the Church. My husband is a minister in another church, I am the pastor of my church, my children are attending parochial school.

I was led to believe my entire life that my ancestry is Scandinavian, and as you can see I am blond and blue-eyed. And yet every time we would attend a family holiday dinner or a life cycle event, it was clear that another part of the family had dark hair and eyes, and other ethnic differences. No one ever explained this to me, and I never really pursued it.

Then, three weeks ago my grandmother, also of fair complexion, who was quite old and dying invited me and my sister to her home. She revealed to us that before she died, she wanted us to know something. Her father, my great grandfather whom I never met, was a Sephardic Jew whose ancestry went back to the Spanish Inquisition. He had practiced his religion with devotion and while he had married a Christian woman of Scandinavian ethnicity, he never gave up his Jewish traditions. And, in fact, his Christian wife, also observed some of these Jewish traditions including Passover, lighting Sabbath candles, and refraining from eating certain non-kosher foods.

These practices were basically done without much fanfare, and once it was clear that I had chosen to become a Christian minister, the entire issue was never discussed again. But now that my grandmother was soon to be called to the Almighty, she felt compelled to reveal the truth to me and my sister. She then took out a box, which she had hidden from us, and showed us its contents which included a Hebrew Bible, Shabbat candlesticks, a Kiddush cup, a Passover Haggadah, and some religious jewelry. Then, she said, Rabbi, I never knew of my Jewish roots before, and I need to ask you to forgive me.

She began to cry again. I told her that there was no need to forgive her, for she didn't do anything wrong. I knew that she was an excellent minister and a fine human being. She continued," You don't understand, Rabbi, my whole life, I have devoted myself to bring people to Christ, and perhaps along the way I may have even brought some Jews to accept Jesus. How could I do this? I have betrayed my own people who had been forced with violence and even by death to give up their Judaism in the past. I have betrayed the Jewish people. Rabbi, please let me come to synagogue on Yom Kippur, so that I can ask God to forgive me for what I have done to my people!"

Once again she cried. I got up from my chair and gave Theresa a hug and tried to assure her that she had nothing to repent for, but if it would help her, she certainly was welcome to come to my synagogue on Yom Kippur. That year Theresa was one of the first people to attend Yom Kippur services and one of the last to leave. Until she moved from El Paso a few years ago, she continued to come to our Yom Kippur worship.

23

We never really discussed the conversation again, except at one time when I met her after one of our interfaith programs. I asked her how she was doing and what she was doing with her knowledge of her Jewish roots. She answered as follows, "Rabbi, thanks for everything, your kindness, your confidentiality, your compassion, and your understanding. As for me, I have made peace with myself and with God. And I continue to do what I do. I just preach a little less New Testament and a lot more Jeremiah." We hugged we smiled, and wished each other well.

Sophie is another person, who had learned of her Jewish roots, started attending services at our synagogue, and came to speak to me personally. Sophie was a social worker, who had lived in Los Angeles where she always felt rejected by the synagogues. She attended both Ashkenazi and Sephardic congregations and discovered that after attending each a few times, the congregants would come and talk with her.

Once they learned that she had been practicing Christianity before discovering that she was a crypto-Jew, they began to question her intentions and made her feel very uncomfortable. In fact, at one synagogue she was told that she was not welcome any more.

When she came to El Paso, she felt the same way at first. She felt unwelcome at my synagogue by my predecessor and also felt uncomfortable at the reform temple. She thanked me for making her feel welcomed. Since she actually felt part of our congregation, she had begun to attend regularly and brought her children as well.

Sophie in many ways became the unofficial leader of the crypto-Jews of El Paso. Many of those who were curious about their Jewish roots would come to her for friendship and advice. We became very close and after a year of study with me, Sophie did her return by coming to the Mikvah and appearing before a *Bet Din* (a Council or Court of Rabbis). She was given a Hebrew name and became even more involved.

We decided to ask the Jewish Federation to allow us to form a support group for B'nei Anusim[1] (i.e. the Children of those who were forced), who were in need of advice and counsel. The Federation agreed and Sophie served as the mentor. The group met once a week for several years at the Jewish Community Center. It was successful, and there were as many as fifteen to twenty people who came to the

---

1   The Hebrew word *anous* means "forced one" or "raped one", implying that crypto-Jews were forced and violated to achieve their conversion to Christianity.

group regularly. Those who attended came from a variety of backgrounds. Some were just curious, but others had done serious research and knew that they were B'nei Anusim. Some were messianic,[2] and still others who weren't sure who they were or what they wanted to do.

Each attendee appreciated the fact that there was a place to talk about their spiritual journey and the path to Judaism. In addition we invited the crypto-Jewish/B'nei Anusim community to have a meal during the festival of Sukkot at my synagogue, Congregation B'nai Zion. We advertised the invitation in our synagogue bulletin, in the Jewish Federation monthly newspaper, and in the *El Paso Times*. Once again, the response was quite good with as many as thirty or forty attending. The members of my congregation were welcoming and supportive.

The B'nei Anusim were appreciative of the warm reception that they were given at our synagogue. I learned many things from Sophie. Since I am not a crypto-Jew, it is hard for me to fully understand their innermost feelings and all of the things that they experienced along the way of their journey back to Judaism. Sophie explained to me that the crypto-Jews were in a unique and delicate situation. Many of them faced constant rejection and humiliation. Christian family members and friends would distant themselves when they learned that the person was thinking about returning to Judaism. After all, even the possibility of returning meant that such a person was possibly giving up a belief in Jesus, which meant they would be going to hell.

2   The term "messianic" refers to people who identify as Christians but add Jewish traditions to their practice.

She reminded me that often the rejection came from the Jewish community, as well. Some Jews would not welcome them at the beginning of their quest, when they first attended a synagogue to simply explore the possibility that they might want to return. Worse still, some Jews wouldn't accept them even after they did a full conversion and return.

Fortunately, these cases of Jewish rejection have become the exception, rather than the rule. But the questioning means that people of crypto-Jewish or anusim backgrounds have to clearly prove their sincerity and genuine interest in reclaiming their Jewish roots. This seems unfair to me. Why shouldn't the mainstream Jewish community be opening their arms in welcoming the anusim?

26

It has been a long journey for many and yet when they are ready to make the return they are sometimes confronted with closed doors and closed arms. This is probably one of the reasons that there are literally just a handful of rabbis in the world who give attention to the B'nei Anusim. When I became involved with the crypto-Jews thirty years ago, I tried to find rabbis and rabbinical organizations that were interested in the subject and found myself with very few positive responses. Over the years, I have met most of the rabbis who support the return of the B'nei Anusim, but they are few in number.

Unfortunately after some illness and personal issues, Sophie has limited her involvement in recent years, but one issue that was particularly of interest to her was that the government of Spain should offer citizenship to the descendants of the Jews who had been forcibly expelled from that country in 1492. I and all the B'nei Anusim owe a deep debt of gratitude to Sophie as one of the local pioneers of the crypto-Jewish/B'nei Anusim movement.

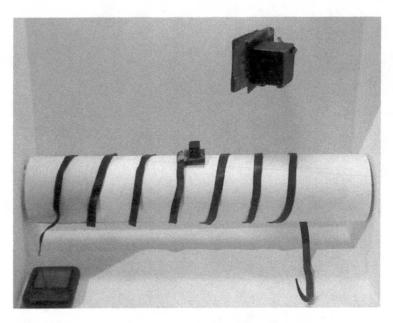

The tefillin given to Rabbi Leon, described in the following chapter, is in the upper right of this photograph from the exhibition "Fractured Faiths: Spanish Judaism, the Inquisition and New World Identities" in 2016 at the New Mexico History Museum. The smaller tefillin shown wrapped is from fifteenth century Spain.

Photo Ron D. Hart.
Courtesy of the New Mexico History Museum

Chapter Two

The Tefillin

ONE OF THE MOST MOVING B'NEI ANUSIM STO-
ries occurred just a few years ago. While sitting
in my office at the synagogue, the secretary told
me that three people had just come in and were anx-
ious to speak with me. Then, in walked an elderly, short
dark haired woman wearing a plain dress, accompanied
by a younger woman, about forty-five-years-old who
was wearing jeans and a brown jacket, and a man in his
mid-forties also in jeans and a blue denim jacket.

Without asking permission the elderly woman took
the seat directly in front of me, and the couple asked permission to sit down. The younger woman, whom I shall
refer to as Beverly, told me that she, her husband Jimmy,
and her mother Maria had spent the last few days in San
Antonio attending her son's graduation from college. The
family lives in Los Angeles, but Maria, who had a terminal
illness, did not like to fly, and so they drove from Los Angeles to San Antonio. They were on their way home traveling along Interstate 10 when Maria told her son-in-law, to
get off the highway and find a synagogue.

Beverly could not understand her mother's request,
because she was a religious Catholic, and it was the first
time she can recall her mother even using the term, "synagogue". Nevertheless, Maria was insistent, and so they
turned off the next exit, which was Exit 13 Sunland Park,

and pulled into the first gas station and asked where the nearest synagogue was located. The attendant directed them to Congregation B'nai Zion, which he knew was on Cherry Hill Lane about two miles from there.

"And now," Beverly said, "we are here, Rabbi, and I don't know why. Mom, tell the Rabbi why we are here." Maria's eyes were old and black and filled with emotion, and she spoke with a deep Spanish accent, "My dear Rabbi," she began and went on to say,

30

I am so grateful that you were willing to speak with me on short notice. I am sure that you are a very busy man. Rabbi, I am eighty-six-years-old and I will die soon, but before I die it is very important that I tell you something. I have practiced the Catholic religion my entire life, as has my family. When I was a little girl living in Mexico, my grandfather invited me into a private room in our house, every single morning but Sabado, *Saturday. And he would place on his arm and his head two black boxes and black straps. He would pray for a few minutes wearing these items, and then he put them away in a blue velvet bag. I was the only family member to witness this event and the only one to know about it.*

When my grandfather was about to die, he called me into his bedroom and revealed to me that he was Jewish, these items were Jewish, and that they had belonged to his grandfather's grandfather from Toledo, Spain and that they were the only remnant of the family's Jewish ancestry. He made me promise to him that somehow, when no one was looking, that I would bury one of these boxes with him, and the other box I would keep and when I was ready to die, I would tell my children, so that they would bury that Jewish box with me. And so, my grandfather passed away many years ago, and I saw to it, that next to him in the coffin, I managed to place that Jewish prayer box.

I haven't slept so well in recent days, dear Rabbi, because I know that I will be in heaven, soon, next to my Saba, as he told me to call him, next to my grandpa. But I shouldn't be buried with my grandfather's other Jewish box. It isn't right, and it isn't fair to him and to his Jewish grandparents. I am not Jewish. I have loved Jesus Christ my entire life. I go to Church every Sunday. I do not want to disrespect my grandfather or the Jewish people. That is why I haven't slept so well, Rabbi.

But then last night after my grandson's graduation I fell asleep for the first time in weeks, and I had a dream. In that dream my grandfather came to me and told me, Maria, I see that you are very troubled by the promise you made to me on my death bed. I will release you from that promise on one condition. You must make me a new promise, that you will find a religious Jew, and you will tell him of your promise to me. If he agrees to promise you that he will bury that religious object with him when he dies, then you can be released from your vow. For then, I will know, you will know, and my Jewish ancestors will know, that this Jewish box will be buried in a Jewish cemetery with a religious Jew and in that way it will surely be returned to our family, who kept it part of us from generation to generation.

She looked directly into my eyes, and we both began to cry. She opened her purse and took out the black box that contains part of the Torah scroll in which the commandment to bind these words upon our arms and between our eyes is found. The beautiful, old, tear-drenched tefillin, was the most beautiful religious item that I had ever held in my hand. She handed it to me and took my hands in hers and asked me to swear to her in her grandfather's name that I would agree to have this tefillin buried with me when I die. I promised her, and I will keep that promise.

That tefillin is always kept nearby me, and I will take it to my grave. With a big sigh of relief, Maria smiled and thanked me, we hugged for a few minutes and said, "Shalom". She left my office, and her daughter and son-in-law remained. Beverly revealed to me that she had no clue about her mother's Jewish background or that she had this Jewish prayer box for over twenty-five years.

Although Beverly was almost speechless, she thanked me for understanding and doing this for her mother. I told her that I was really the one to thank her for bringing Maria to me, and that maybe it was really God that had arranged the meeting. I further told her that I wasn't doing this just for her mother, but for the generations and generations of Jews who had given blood, pain, and their very lives to keep Judaism alive.

I thanked God for her mother and told her that this meeting was not just a coincidence, but as it is said in Yiddish, "Beshert". It was "destiny" that made this meeting happen. As I reflect on this incident, I really believe that this was not just a coincidence. Maria lives in Los

Angeles where there are hundreds of rabbis, and yet she had never said a word about her Jewish ancestry until this moment. How did she just happen to stop in El Paso, at the exit on the highway where my synagogue is located, and come to me, a rabbi, who has devoted a good part of his life welcoming the B'nei Anusim home?

The sacred tefillin of Maria's grandfather is connected to the past history of the crypto-Jews from the time of the Inquisition and is also connected to the future generations of the crypto-Jews who continue to return every day. The tefillin are worn on the arm, so that we will make a physical commitment to follow the commandments, and they are worn between the eyes, so that we will think with devotion and dedication as the reasons why this commitment must be from the depths of our hearts. For the crypto-Jew it is the same. The sincere return inspires a physical action, to become involved in performing the rituals and customs which were forcibly taken from them generations ago, and it also requires learning the meaning of the Torah, the rituals, and the Mitzvot which identifies them with their Jewish ancestors and the Jewish progeny to come. Like the tefillin of Maria's grandfather, the commitment of the B'nei Anusim is bound by each arm and mind.

Portuguese Synagogue in Amsterdam
Photo Vanessa Paloma Elbaz

Chapter Three

My Visit To Belmonte, Portugal

N THE SUMMER OF 1999 I WAS GIVEN A RARE OP-
portunity to visit many of the places where Jews had
traveled after the expulsion from Spain. The ultimate
goal was to visit Belmonte, Portugal where I had learned
that some 200 crypto-Jews had converted in the twen-
tieth century, making their return to Judaism. The first
place on my journey was Amsterdam.

My wife and I visited the famous Portuguese Synagogue in Amsterdam and read of the history of that house
of worship that was built in 1675 by a rabbi, who was born
to an anusim family in Portugal and later made his way
to this city to return to Judaism and study to be a rabbi.
We met one of the actual descendants of those Spanish ancestors whose name was Mr. Pereira. He told of how welcoming the people of Amsterdam were and how well they
treated the early conversos who were desperately looking
for a new home.

He gave a brief history of that beautiful synagogue
which was dedicated in the seventeenth century. He also
said that he did not know of any crypto-Jews living in
Amsterdam today, that by this time every one was either
Jewish or Catholic. As he was giving us his lecture and
tour, a group of yeshiva students came into the synagogue. They, too, were visiting the inspiring edifice.

Suddenly, they broke into song, in Yiddish, Hebrew and Ladino, and they sang with a wonderful
spirit, passion, and joy. It was such a moving experience for us. I couldn't help but envision the first Jewish children, who found their home in this community
and might have sung the same prayers and melodies
500 years ago. I really felt their spiritual company es-
corting me on my journey, which in all probability was
their journey, as well.

We also visited the Jewish community of Barcelona, Spain. In one building we found that the lower floor
housed the Sephardic synagogue and in the upper floor
there was a Chabad Hasidic synagogue. I spoke at length
with both rabbis about the anusim in Spain.

Each rabbi knew of members of their respective congregations who had been aware of their hidden Jewish
family background, but there were only two or three over
the many years. In each case, they had made a full conversion after a year of study, and they were accepted as
Jews in the congregation. In reality, however, they did
not experience, the same phenomenon that I was experi-
encing in El Paso. They were fascinated by my story but
couldn't really identify with it.

In Barcelona, like Amsterdam, one was either a Jew or
a Christian. They did direct me to an area in Barcelona,
which had been the Jewish Quarter until 1391 when it was
attacked, and Jews were either killed, converted, or fled for
their lives. Other than street names, there are no signs of
Jewish history or current Jewish presence when we were
there. Later, I have learned that the location one of the old

synagogues was identified and is now open, and a small Jewish Museum has been established.

From Barcelona we flew to Palma, Majorca where I had learned of the presence of a crypto-Jewish community called *chuetas*. I learned about the *chuetas* of Palma from a video tape that I purchased in Jerusalem a year before this visit.

It was a historical video made by the former late President of Israel, Yitzhak Navon, entitled, "Out of Spain 1492". It is an excellent presentation that covers the different places where anti-Semitism in the form of attacks on communities and the Inquisition raised its ugly head in the Iberian Peninsula. We learned of the terrible persecution of the Jews of Majorca in 1391, where virtually every Jew either converted to Christianity or lost their life.

When the Inquisitors returned in 1691 there were virtually no Jews left. The Navon film tells about the mayor of Palma, who knew that he had Jewish ancestry and that he was a *chueta*. The film includes an incident in a Catholic parochial school in Palma where a student was playing soccer and accidentally caused his opponent to trip. Suddenly, the injured student called the one who tripped him, "a dirty *chueta*". The student ran to the priest in protest for the name-calling and did not know what the term *chueta* meant.

Later, he learned that the term was similar to *marrano* or pig and that it came from the history of the crypto-Jews in Majorca. During the Inquisition, one of the practices that the anusim observed, which would endanger their lives, was abstaining from eating pork. The Majorcan dialect for pork is "*choyto*" and the crypto-Jews would eat a suckling pig in public in order to save their lives. Hence the term *chueta* became a derogatory term for crypto-Jews.

In the film, I also learned of another one of my heroes, Rabbi Nissan ben Avraham, who was a *chueta* from Majorca. He had been a practicing Catholic, and his Christian name was Nicholas Aguilo. When Nicholas learned that he had Jewish roots, he started studying about Judaism. Ultimately he went to Israel where he converted and then studied to become a rabbi. He was ordained by the Chief Rabbinate in Jerusalem and since has written two books about the B'nei Anusim.

One of his books entitled, *Els Anussim,* discusses the halachic, or Jewish legal requirements for B'nei Anusim to return to Judaism. Rabbi Nissan presently lives in Shilo, Israel where he is a scribe, a teacher, and a guide. The Navon film shows Rabbi Nissan on *Yom Atzmaut* at an observance in Jerusalem in 1992 on the occasion of the 500th anniversary of the expulsion of the Jews from Spain. He was given the privilege of lighting the last candle during that observance. As he kindled the light, Rabbi Nissan, the first of the B'nei Anusim, to be an ordained rabbi in Israel, proclaimed that he was not only lighting the candle for the State of Israel, but also for all of the B'nei Anusim in every corner of the globe. He honored those who continue to light candles in darkness as they commit themselves to "Hatikvah", which is the national anthem of Medinat Yisrael and which means "Hope".

This moment in Navon's film is one of the most poignant and dramatic moments I have ever experienced. I had the privilege of meeting Rabbi Nissan in 2008 when

I led a B'nei Anusim tour of Israel, on which I brought twenty-nine people, among whom were seventeen of crypto-Jewish ancestry. We heard Rabbi Nissan's story when we were visiting Tel Aviv, and then I invited him to be the keynote speaker for our annual Anusim conference in El Paso. Rabbi Nissan gave a brilliant presentation and brought with him a detailed family tree of 500 years of the history of his Catholic, Jewish, and crypto-Jewish family that his brother had compiled. I will talk further of Rabbi Nissan ben Avraham in a later chapter.

39

When I visited Palma in 1999, I was looking for "The Street of the Silversmiths", "*Calle Platerias*", which was shown in Navon's film. Unfortunately, the city had officially changed the name to *Calle Argentina*, but since I had an older map, I was able to locate the street. I went into a book store asking the salesperson if he had any books about the *chuetas*. He literally asked me to leave the store, as if the subject was not to be discussed.

A short while later, I was near a large Catholic Church, and I found a small book store which I entered with a little trepidation. I again asked for a book about *chuetas*. To my surprise and delight, the saleslady very kindly brought me a copy of Rabbi Nissan's, *Els Anussim*. I gladly purchased it and then asked the girl if she could show me the Street of the Silversmiths. She asked another salesperson to watch the shop and took me to the street which was only a few blocks from the store. Although the official street sign read "*Calle Argentina*", I found written in chalk on one of the walls on the street, the words, "*Calle Platerias*". I was really excited and decided that now I would go into one of the shops and find someone who would tell me about the B'nei Anusim of Palma.

Without much success in the first three shops, I came into a smaller shop, and I noticed that on the corner of the doorpost there appeared to be the outline of what might have once been a Mezuzah. I decided to enter that particular store and take my chances.

I told the young man in that shop that I wanted to find out about the *chuetas*. He replied that if I bought something in his shop, he would give me some information. It was sort of a bribe, and so I responded by saying that if he gave me some Jewish jewelry I would agree. He smiled and told me to wait a minute. He went into the back of the shop and brought me a small silver Jewish Star. I purchased it and thanked him.

He began to tell me about this street and that at one time most of the apartments and shops had been owned by Jews, but after the Inquisition, there really weren't any Jews left. He said that there was some talk that the present owners of the shops on the street today were part of the *chuetas* but wouldn't admit to it, and that no one that he knew actually practiced Judaism today.

At that moment, his father walked into the store, saw the Jewish Star that I had purchased became angry at his son and told me to please leave his store. It was clear to me that anyone who had Jewish ancestry living in Palma, Majorca was not willing to talk about it and did not welcome anyone who was interested in the subject. I left Palma with mixed feelings. I was glad that I had come there, found the *Calle Platerias*, the book by Rabbi Nissan, and that I had purchased the Jewish Star, but I was sad that apparently the Jewish community of Palma had all but disappeared.

The next place on my journey was Lisbon. I visited the Plaza de Rossi where I learned that in 1506 two thousand Jews had been killed in horrific ways in the Lisbon massacre. Today, in the plaza there are shops and restaurants, but not one memorial or mention of the Jews who were slaughtered there simply because they were Jews.

We need to remember that these decisions to kill people of Jewish heritage were made, not by Nazis, but by religious leaders of the Catholic Church, who believed in Jesus, who was Jewish. What a sad chapter in the history of the Church. My ancestors were the victims of their barbarism, and their ancestors were the perpetrators of perhaps the worst crimes in the history of religion, and to this day, they remain silent and show no remorse.

When crypto-Jews were burned at the stake, if they would confess and accept Jesus as Lord, then the executioner would garrote (i.e. strangle) the person preventing the pain of the being burned alive. The crypto-Jew who refused to confess, would be burned alive, the victim of excruciating pain.

In the Plaza de Rossi, I put on my yarmulke and chanted loudly the *El Malei Rachamim*, the Hebrew memorial prayer for the dead, followed by the Mourner's Kaddish. I was not going to leave that place without paying homage to the memory of my Jewish family. The next day I talked with the Rabbi in Lisbon, who had only been there a few years. I learned about the Jewish community of Lisbon and was told that the crypto-Jews in Lisbon were not a factor. He said that people were either open about their Jewish identity or retained their Catholic identity. In subsequent conversations with individual B'nei Anusim, who lived in Portugal and who contacted me, I learned that the synagogues in Lisbon do not welcome people of anusim backgrounds and are not interested in reaching out to them or accepting them.

I also spoke to the Rabbi about the community of Belmonte, which I was planning to visit for two days. He told me that he had heard about this community, but that he had not visited Belmonte and wasn't planning to. I was disappointed in his attitude and realized that this was a journey that I needed to make by myself. Besides learning about the Plaza de Rossi, it is also important to learn a little about the anusim history in Portugal.

After the expulsion of the Jews from Spain in 1492, King John of Portugal invited them to find refuge in his country. A few years later, his successor, King Manuel, wanted to marry the daughter of King Ferdinand and Queen Isabella. They told him that if he wanted to marry their daughter he would have to expel the Jews from his country. He began to comply with their demands.

The first act was to forcibly baptize thousands of Jewish children and take them away from their parents to be raised by Christian families. This was followed by the Edict of Expulsion of Jews from Portugal. In order to save their lives and Jewish identity, many Jews left the country or moved to remote areas of Portugal far from the capital. As the deadline for leaving Portugal drew near, the remaining Jews were ordered to report to Lisbon where they were subjected to a mass baptism and declared Christians. Their descendants are B'nei Anusim, the children of those who were forced. Over the last century Jewish communities were found to have existed in Porto, Guarda, Belmonte, and other towns.

In 1995 I had met Rabbi Joseph Stampfer of Portland, Oregon at a conference for the Society of Crypto-Jewish Studies in El Paso when he spoke about his visit to Belmonte. After the talk, I told him of my working with the crypto-Jews of the Southwest and of my desire to visit Belmonte. He told me that the community was reluctant to give out much information and referred me to a book called *The Last Crypto Jews of Portugal*,[3] which gives the story of the crypto-Jews of Belmonte.

43

I learned that in 1917 a Jewish businessman, Samuel Schwarz, decided to explore business opportunities in Portugal. He had learned about areas that might have commercial potential, and with that in mind, he set out to visit them. He was unaware that in the area there was the community of Belmonte that had families who had maintained their Jewish identity from the sixteenth century.

After traveling through many of the small villages in northeast he arrived to Belmonte. In the course of his discussions with some of the members of the community, who were all outwardly Catholic, he inadvertently blurted out a Jewish expression such as *Baruch Hashem*. Suddenly one of the people who was doing business with him said that the expression sounded familiar and asked what the words meant. Then, the person said a version of *"Sh'ma Yisrael Adony Eloheinu Adonye Echad."* Schwarz asked where he had learned those words. The man replied, "O many of us have been saying these words every morning and every evening, but we don't know their meaning."

3   David A Canelo, *Last Crypto Jews of Portugal*. Judaica Press. 1990.

Schwarz explained to the man that this was the basic prayer and proclamation of the Jewish people coming from the Book of Deuteronomy in the Torah and that the words translated, "Hear, O Israel, the Lord is our God, the Lord is One." When the man heard the translation, he began to cry and told Sam that these words have been in his family and in the families of many of the residents of Belmonte for centuries.

44   In the decades following the visit of Mr. Schwarz, the B'nei Anusim of Belmonte made the radical step of returning to their roots. They began reading and studying about Judaism by themselves and eventually brought in a rabbi from Israel to work with them. In the process, they built a synagogue, and some 200 residents made conversion with a visiting rabbi from Israel. They were trying to get one of their own to go to Israel, study to be a rabbi, and return to lead the community. My visit to Belmonte was in 1999, and it was the day after I spoke with the Rabbi in Lisbon, who expressed no interest in these people, who had survived for centuries with the memory of their Jewish heritage.

I knew that the success or failure of my trip would depend on whether or not I would be able to meet with the leaders of the Jewish community, but there was no way to contact them until I actually arrived in the town. I was given a few names and phone numbers, but I didn't know if they would talk with me. I was warned that there was some turmoil within the community, and that the leaders were not trustful of outsiders and might not be willing to talk with me as a stranger.

I made a reservation at the Belsol Hotel in Belmonte, and I had a tape recorder, camera and video camera with me. I left from Lisbon early in the morning, and I estimated that it would take me about four or five hours to get there. Everything was going well, and then with about an hour or so to go, the highway abruptly ended. No warning, no signs, I just followed the traffic on side roads. I don't speak Portuguese, and there was no place to stop and ask directions.

After about forty-five minutes on back roads, I came into a town, and stopped by a gas station. With map in hand, my broken Spanish and the gas attendants very broken English, I was relieved to know that Belmonte was only about twenty-five minutes away.

I followed the man's directions, and forty minutes later I entered the town of Belmonte. I saw signs to the hotel and to the synagogue, and I decided first to scout out the synagogue area. One of the things that was quickly apparent to me was that after turning off the main road, many of the side roads didn't have signs identifying the name of the street. It also appeared to me that the synagogue, which was quaint, new, and beautiful, was not in a nice section of town. Although most of the occupants of Belmonte seemed to own stores or small businesses, I didn't see the affluent part of the town.

The synagogue was locked, and so I decided to go to the hotel. When I got to my room, I dialed the phone numbers that I had been given but got no answers. I thought that I would go back to the synagogue and wait there, but I wasn't sure that was such a good idea. I asked the proprietor of the hotel to help me, and he told me to wait a minute.

A few minutes later he brought me the phone, and there was a woman's voice on the other end. With the help of the hotel clerk, I was able to convey to the woman that I was a rabbi from Texas, and that I wanted to see the synagogue and visit the Jewish community. Evidently she was one of the teachers and one of the heads of the Belmonte Jewish congregation. She gave me directions to her home, and a few minutes later we left the hotel.

As we followed the written directions to her house, I realized that I was lost, that there were no street signs, and that I had no phone number to call. I put on my yarmulke and passed a few children on the road. I said, "Shalom" and thank God, they responded, "Shalom".

I said, "*Morah*", the Hebrew word for "teacher". They smiled and gestured for me to follow them. A few moments later I parked in front of an old, white house which evidently was the correct location. My wife and I walked up the path to the front door, which had a mezuzah on the door post, and I knew that we were at the right place. I will call the woman "Rosa Moreno" since she made me promise not to use her real name. She also would not allow me to video, record, or take pictures of her or her family. She seemed to still have a bit of the "Inquisition" mentality and was afraid that her Jewish identity would be revealed.

Communication was challenging, my broken Spanish, her fluent Portuguese, our mutual Hebrew, and her limited English did allow us to converse. She introduced us to her children and brought us orange juice and cookies. The entire house was filled with Jewish things. Menorahs, Chanukiot, Kiddush cups, Hebrew books, prayer books, and Bibles, needlepoint, paintings, a small map of Israel were in every corner of the small house. We talked for over two hours about the Jews of Belmonte. She took me to the synagogue of which she so proud. I was allowed to take photos on the outside, but not on the inside. She also showed me another place where there had been a mezuzah on the door where the Jewish community used to gather in secret.

She also explained that some people go to synagogue on Shabbat, and yet also attend Church on Sunday, not because they believe in Christianity, but because they don't trust their Christian neighbors. She told me that she was afraid to be photographed or taped because once before without her knowledge someone had taken her picture as the head of the Jewish community, and the next thing she knew it appeared in a local newspaper. She also stated that while she refused to be on an audio tape, she had a neighbor who loved to sing and crocheted challah covers, and that this neighbor would agree to allow us to tape her singing.

We went to Hannah's house and sat at the table, and we bought one her beautiful challah covers. Then, I sang "Shalom Aleichem" to her. In turn, she sang in Portuguese her version of the melody to "Hatikvah", the national anthem of Israel. After we left the community having such an inspiring visit, I told Mrs. Moreno that my synagogue in El Paso would help her community in any way that we could. We would send books, we would send records, educational supplies, even financial support. Her response to me, I will never forget, "Send us a rabbi". That was the one thing I could not do.

When I returned to Texas after this incredible visit, I did try to identify a young rabbi through rabbinical schools and organizations, but my search was unsuccessful. Later, I received reports from Yaakov Gladstone, of blessed memory, that they were continuing to look for a rabbi, and it is my prayer that one day their dream will be fulfilled. Although he could not find a rabbi, Yaakov did recruit Vanessa Paloma to go to Belmonte as a teacher for the women and children, and she taught them Sephardic songs and Jewish domestic practices that had been lost. Later, Yaakov received a lifetime award from Kulanu for his work with the anusim.

Chapter Four

The Return Of the B'nei Anusim
As Part of God's Divine Plan

I HAVE OFTEN BEEN ASKED WHY I AM SO PASSIONATE about the return of the B'nei Anusim.[4] Let me share this very spiritual moment in my life. At the beginning of my journey when I was first meeting and talking to people with crypto-Jewish[5] background I had a conversation with God. I am aware that this may sound very strange, so let me assure you, that it was unusual for me, as well, and remember that I am a rabbi. Actually, the first part of the dialogue was not that remarkable, many people speak to God, but the fact that God responded was very special and unique.

Let me describe what happened. I said to the Almighty,

> *Dear God, you have kept your promises to the Jewish people. You told us that, 'I will dwell among you.' And it is true, if we seek, we will find You. I know You are a personal God. You commanded Abraham to go to the Land of Israel, and Israel today is our*

4   The Children of those who were converted by force in Spain by the forces of the Church and the Inquisition. *B'nai* - children and *Anusim* - the forced ones.

5   The term crypto-Jews refers to those who converted to Christianity under pressure and continued to practice Judaism in hiding.

homeland, strong and vibrant. You made a covenant with the Jewish people and gave us the Ten Commandments and the Torah, which today are still the guiding laws of our people. On the other hand, You told us that we would be as numerous as the stars in the heavens and the sands of the sea.

God, I continued, That is not true. In fact there are fewer Jews in the world today then existed in 1939. God why did you not fulfill your promise?

50

God responded. Now when I say that "God responded" I can't actually describe how I received the Lord's message. I can't say that the Almighty spoke to me in the same manner that human beings communicate with each other. In fact, I am unable to describe exactly how God's words came to me. It was not in a dream or in a vision, nevertheless, in some Divine way I received the following message,

Yes, it is true, but I did not build the concentration camps, nor the crematoria or gas chambers, the Nazis did evil to the Jewish people, and I cannot bring back the sacred souls of the beloved six million of our people who were murdered. I weep with you.

However, some 500 years earlier another group of people committed acts of brutality, torture, even burning My people alive at the stake, and this time they claimed that this was done in My name. I cannot forgive them for what they did, but most of those people were not exterminated. Many survived, but they were forced through violent and heinous crimes to give up their faith. Those people are alive today, they may have been lost to Judaism temporarily, but they continue to carry on their faith secretly, and millions of their descendants are alive today, and you need to reach out to them and help them return. Once they do, you will be as numerous as the sands of the sea and the stars in the sky.

This conversation with God has remained with me to this day, and I believe that it is true. Many years ago, I was at a lecture about Jewish survival, and the speaker was a Jewish sociologist who estimated that if it were not for the Holocaust, there would be approximately 40 million Jews in the world today instead of about 14 million. I started doing research on the status of the world Jewish population today if the Inquisition never happened. At the caucus on crypto-Jews held at the Knesset in Israel October 2016, Ashley Perry, the director of Reconectar, an organization that facilitates a reconnection with the descendants of Spanish and Portuguese Jewish communities, gave a lecture in which he stated that there are over 100 million people in the world today who have Sephardic Jewish roots. Imagine what an impact the return of even a small percentage of those potential returnees to Judaism would have on the Jewish people and the world at large. I see the return of the anusim as the fulfillment of God's promise to Abraham.

The subject of crypto-Jews and B'nei Anusim is not well known and needs to be studied, discussed, and disseminated, specifically within Jewish communities for its impact will have a profound effect on the Jewish people for many generations to come. First, it is necessary to understand the term "crypto-Jew". Originally, the word used to describe Jews in hiding was *marranos*, which is a derogatory term meaning pigs or swine. Other words that have been used to describe secret Jews are *conversos* and *anusim*, but each of these terms refers to the same people.

52   During the Spanish Inquisition, thousands upon thousands of Jews were forcibly converted to Christianity by the ruthlessness of the Catholic Church, directed by the grand inquisitor Torquemada and others and funded primarily by Queen Isabella and King Ferdinand. The goal of the Inquisition was to root out and eliminate Jewish and Muslim beliefs and other so called heresies within Christendom. In order to carry out this plan a number of methods were used including horrific torture devices, death penalties, forced confessions, testimonies of neighbors who were rewarded in many ways for their evidence, confiscation of property, expulsion, and ultimately being burned alive at the stake.

The documentation of these barbaric tactics is recorded in the works of Cecil Roth, Ben Zion Netanyahu, Chaim Beinart, and other scholars who have studied this history. The initial target of the Inquisition was those Jews who had converted to Christianity in order to save their lives and the lives of their children and family members. Although they publicly converted to Christianity, many continued to practice Jewish rituals and traditions in secret. By converting, they were often able to save their lives in the face of threats and even torture.

On the other hand, at the risk of being discovered and possibly becoming victims of further torture and death, thousands of Jews hid their identity by secretly preserving Jewish traditions. For example, many Jewish women would light candles on Friday night in a dark, back room of their homes. At public feasts, many Jews would refrain from eating pork. While going to Church on Sundays, certain Jews would take jobs where they would not have to work on Saturday. If they did work on their Sabbath, they would wear nicer clothes in honor of the sanctity of the Jewish day of rest.

These deviations from normal Christian practice could put their lives at risk, for the Church rewarded informers, who would notify priests, if they noticed someone who refused to eat pork, or wore special Saturday clothing, or would act in any way that seemed to imply a Jewish custom. This accusation could result in torture and death for the person and confiscation of their property. There is evidence that conversos would gather in small groups on Yom Kippur, the most important Jewish holy day and recite the Kol Nidre prayer, asking God to forgive them for their conversion to Christianity, which they had accepted in order to save their lives. While thousands of Jews kept their Judaism secretly, thousands also died for attempting to conceal their Jewish identity.

Following the expulsion of Jews from Spain and the subsequent oppression of Jews in Portugal after 1497, they migrated to many countries that would accept them, creating the Sephardic Diaspora. Over the centuries that followed, conversos and crypto-Jews either returned to Judaism in the Netherlands, Italy, Morocco, and the Ottoman Empire, or they migrated to Spanish territories in South America, the Azores, Canary Islands, Curaçao, Mexico, and the Southwest of the United States. Today, five hundred years after the fateful day of that expulsion in 1492, descendants of anusim, the 'B'nei Anusim' are returning to their Jewish roots.

The Jews of Spain, who gave up their Judaism under the threat of death, were not true converts. According to the architects of the Inquisition in the Catholic church, it was ordered and promulgated in the name of God, so it is important to understand now that the return of the B'nei Anusim must also be part of God's divine plan. Forced conversions, torturing innocent human beings, who have not committed any crime, burning human beings alive at the stake are examples of ungodly, despicable, violent acts. Persons and institutions that collude to commit such atrocities must be held accountable for their actions and suffer the consequences of their barbarism.

The reality is that there have not been any real penalties for the evil acts of the Inquisition upon the anusim. To this day, the Catholic church has not assumed responsibility comparable to its actions in this chapter of history. With the exception of a relatively lukewarm apology offered by Pope John Paul II, the Church and the Spanish Crown have remained largely silent regarding these violent actions that they took against the Jews of Spain and its territories. In fact, the history of anti-Semitic actions, including the blood libels of the middle ages, the burning of synagogues, the papal edicts against Jews, has been practiced for centuries and yet the silence of the Church regarding these matters is morally unacceptable.

It seems to me, the return of the crypto-Jews or B'nei Anusim to Judaism today, affords the Catholic Church the opportunity to show remorse for the way it forcibly converted their Jewish ancestors and to apologize for violating the third commandment, which they dishonored 500 years ago. As a religious institution that honors these commandments, the Church must atone for what it did.

The return of the B'nei Anusim today should not only be recognized by the Church, but it should be encouraged to rectify the sins of the generations of the Inquisition that have been ignored.

Let me share a personal experience that illustrates this point. A few years ago, I was invited to talk about Judaism in a local Christian church in El Paso, by a minister whom I met during an interfaith radio program on which we appeared together with a Catholic priest. After the program, the minister and I had lunch together and would occasionally talk on the phone. We developed a cordial, friendly relationship.

Soon thereafter he invited me to speak about Judaism at his church. After my talk, I took my seat in the congregation and listened to the pastor's sermon, which ultimately spoke about sin and atonement and concluded with his asking the Jewish people to forgive Christians for not doing enough to stop the Holocaust. While he was speaking, the minister became very emotional and began to shed some tears.

At that point, he wanted me to respond to his plea and offer my willingness to accept his apology. I didn't

55

know what to do and felt very uncomfortable by his request, and so I just simply sat silently in my seat. But
then, his wife brought a microphone to me and urged me
to respond. I took the microphone and said,

> *Pastor, I truly appreciate your kindness and your
> remorse, but I am not in any position to accept your
> apology. First of all, you really didn't personally do
> anything that I am aware of to promote the evil of
> Nazism, and secondly, I never personally lost anyone
> in the Holocaust, so how can I forgive you on their
> behalf. I would suggest that you find a Holocaust sur-
> vivor, whom I could direct you to, and apologize to
> him directly. All I can do is to thank you for your
> kind words, and for offering me the opportunity to
> speak at your congregation today.*

56

This seemed to satisfy the pastor and his wife, and the
service continued to its conclusion. Following the service
I had the opportunity to have refreshments with the pastor and his congregants. It was then that I decided that
I would invite the pastor to lunch for the sole purpose
of hearing his response to the work that I was doing in
bringing back crypto-Jews to Judaism. A few days later
we had lunch and during the course of the meal I asked
the minister the following question,

> *If a congregant of yours came to you and told you
> that he had recently learned that he had Jewish roots
> and that he had evidence that his family had once
> practiced Judaism, and now, he wanted to explore*

*that Jewish past by going to a synagogue, speaking
to a rabbi, and studying about Judaism, what would
you say to the congregant?*

Without interrupting his salad, he said very non-chalantly, "I would tell that congregant that it is not the Christian thing to do." Somewhat surprised and disappointed, I asked, "Why would you discourage that parishioner?" The pastor answered,

*Because if he did discover these Jewish roots, and
if he ultimately gave up Christianity, he would also
be giving up salvation. The possibility of this happening, is against the teachings of my church and I could
not allow that to happen.*

I thanked the pastor for his frankness, but at the same time, I said to myself, "You bigot! How dare you deny a man the opportunity to simply explore the possibility of returning to his Judaism that was forcibly taken from him in the first place!" Unfortunately, the attitude of this minister is consistent, I believe, with the preoccupation that Christianity has with salvation and the belief that only those who embrace Jesus as their Savior will be saved.

There are those in the Christian religious community who would view it to be a sin for crypto-Jews to return. On the other hand, a few months later while doing research on crypto-Jews in Amsterdam, Italy, Spain, and Portugal, I was given an audience with the Cardinal of Paris Jean Marie Lustiger, thanks to the efforts of my friend, Monsignor Frank Smith, of St. Raphael's Church in El Paso.

I had heard a great deal about Cardinal Lustiger and read his auto-biography. The Cardinal was born to Jewish parents and his mother died in Auschwitz. I also learned that he was involved in improving relationships between the Roman Catholic Church and the Jewish community. It was important for me to hear from Cardinal Lustiger about his views regarding the return of the crypto-Jews. My wife Sharon and I spoke with the good Cardinal for approximately thirty minutes. He had heard of my work with the B'nei Anusim, and we talked about it. He also mentioned that he still had "*mishpacha*", which is the Hebrew word for "family," and that he had attended a family Bar Mitzvah in California.

58

When I asked Jean Marie Lustiger the same question that I had asked the pastor from the Christian Church in El Paso, his response was completely different. Cardinal Lustiger said to me without any hesitation, "I would tell such a congregant who wanted to explore his Jewish roots, 'let God direct you on the proper path.'" The answer of Cardinal Lustiger reassured me that helping the B'nei Anusim was something that even the Church would not find objectionable.

The response of Cardinal Lustiger gave me reassurance because it has never been my goal to alienate or bring rejection to those B'nei Anusim, who come to me for counsel or guidance. These conversations that I had with Christian clergymen regarding the return of the crypto-Jews indicates that there are strong feelings on both sides of the argument.

Only time will ultimately tell how the Christian and Jewish worlds will handle this return, for I am convinced that as more people learn about the story of the B'nei Anusim, more descendants of secret Jews will be exploring their roots. There is no way to predict how small or how large the return will be, but one thing is sure and that is that it is happening today, and it is beginning to effect the religious community. I am convinced that the return of the crypto-Jews is certainly part of God's divine plan, if it weren't, it would not be happening in such large numbers.

59

Part Two

The Anusim and Judaism

Chapter Five

The Third Commandment

I HAVE ALWAYS BEEN FASCINATED BY THE THIRD MANdate of the Ten Commandments that God gave to Moses on Mt. Sinai. It is, "And thou shall not take the name of the Lord thy God in vain. For he that takes the name of the Lord thy God in vain shall not be held guiltless." It is interesting that this is the only commandment that has such a stipulation included in its instruction.

Why is this provision mentioned in this commandment and what do the words, "for he that takes the name of the Lord shall not be held guiltless" actually mean? Is there a particular lesson that we are expected to learn from the terms of this commandment? Why are there consequences added to the third commandment that don't appear in any of the other nine? I believe that the special stipulation in this commandment signals something important about its practice.

First of all, let's analyze the real meaning of the words, "And thou shall not take the name of the Lord your God in vain." Typically most observers conclude that the intention of this commandment is to prohibit us from telling a lie when we have used God's name as some kind of a sacred guarantee for telling the truth. In other words, we are forbidden from making the statement, "I swear to God" if we don't intend on being honest. The second explanation that is equally popular is that one should never curse using the word of God. In other words, the term "goddamnit" is unacceptable because it is blaspheming the name of the Lord by using His name disrespectfully. One other possibility which comes to mind is that we should not dare to speak for God.

When an individual says to others that God is actually telling him to perform a particular act, this can be quite dangerous. For example, a person can say that God told me to blow myself up in His name in order for me to take my life and hundreds of lives of other human beings, and thus give God the culpability for the action. This is an example of taking God's name in vain. In fact, this third example, I am convinced, is the most dangerous way of "taking the name of God in vain" for it holds God and not the perpetrator accountable for the act.

The word translated as "take" means "say" or "speak" to most of us. One should not say the name of God in vain, or one should not speak God's name in vain. But the Hebrew word "*tisa*" actually means "carry" or "take", implying a physical action, as opposed to a verbal expression. It is important to understand the Hebrew translation to comprehend what the text is trying to teach us.

I was at a lecture once by the author and radio personality Dennis Prager, and I recall that he explained the word "*tisa*" to mean "carry", as opposed to "say". After all, when we examine the consequences of "*tisa*", we see that this is the only commandment in which, God says, "I will not hold that person guiltless who takes the name of God in vain." In other words, this is a pretty serious crime. Let's think about it. God is a forgiving God, therefore why would God not forgive the person who only "said" His name in vain.

In commandments that follow the third, there are no such consequences. For violating the Sabbath, for not honoring parents, for murder, stealing, bearing false witness, committing adultery, and for coveting, there is not a similar penalty. Why only in the case of "taking" God's name, will God not be forgiving? In order to answer the question, we first have to understand what it means to "take" or to "carry" God's name. I believe that the commandment is not referring to a verbal activity such as "talking" or "saying" God's name, but rather it is referring to the person who physically "carries" or "takes" the name of the Lord.

It seems to me that such a person is one who actually carries the banner of God through his or her work or actions. A member of the clergy, such as a priest, a minister, a rabbi, an imam, a nun, a cantor, a monk, or any spiritual leader who leads a church, synagogue, mosque, or any other place of worship, portrays himself or herself as "carrying the banner" of the Lord. In addition to persons, who have these official titles as clergy, there are other individuals whose dress or customs represent themselves to be "religious" individuals.

A person who wears a particular head covering in the Jewish or Muslim faith or wears fringes on his garments, or wears the attire of the Amish or Mennonite faiths portrays himself to be one who represents the teachings of God. Another example is someone who attends synagogue or church regularly and follows those traditions and customs with such piety that everyone in the com-

63

munity recognizes that individual as a religious person. These clerics and lay leaders depict themselves to be spokesmen or representatives of the Lord.

If this is so, if such "religious" representatives of God are the subjects described in the third commandment, then why would God not be forgiving to them should they go astray? Of all people, wouldn't God have a soft spot in His heart for them, more so than those who appear to be indifferent in the way that they approach the Almighty?

I believe that if we just read the text of the third commandment the answer will be found. The clergy, spiritual leader or religiously observant individual is actually more accountable to God because he is mentioned in the commandment itself. Such a person is "taking" God's name and therefore is obliged to act godly. He cannot take his religious responsibility to God lightly or without consequences.

It is specifically such a religious person, more than anyone else, who owes it to the Lord to be holy in his moral behavior all the time, because the rest of the community, the world, and God Himself are relying on him or her, to portray God in a sacred, praiseworthy, and ethical light. It is this "religious representative" that God is addressing in the third commandment.

Furthermore, it is specifically because this person "carries" God's name symbolically, that the weight of his or her actions results in such a severe penalty, one in which God will not hold him "guiltless". It is when a so-called religious person acts despicably, immorally, or inappropriately that such an individual brings shame to religion and to God. The hypocritical or unethical behavior of religious people often leads the rest of humanity to view religion as a sham and belief in God as nonsense. It is bad enough when an average person lies or cheats, but when a religious person does so, the rest of the world takes notice and often becomes disenchanted with religion and the Lord. Let me offer some examples to illustrate this point.

Many years ago an Orthodox rabbi wearing a yarmulke was convicted of the crime of cheating hundreds of elderly people, many of them Jews, of the services they had paid for at nursing homes that he directed. This supposed religious man mistreated the residents of these nursing homes and was sent to prison for this despicable crime. Once the sentence was announced, rather than show any remorse for the crime, the rabbi was only concerned with the availability of kosher food in prison for himself. I was a rabbinical student at the time of his sentencing, and I felt deeply ashamed for the religious community and the rabbinate. As a religious person representing the teachings of God, he brought shame to those teachings. I am sure that many people took notice of the religious hypocrisy that this rabbi showed to the entire world. This is the type of person who is being chastised by the word of God in the third commandment.

We are also aware of the television evangelists who have been lecturing millions of people on the importance of following the teachings of Jesus, and then reporters or investigators reveal the disgusting sexual escapades in which they have been involved. How dare they be such hypocrites! They are so judgmental of their television congregants in their "holier than thou" approach to sermonizing, and the next thing we know; they have been exposed to be charlatans and phonies in their sexual and moral lives.

Once again, through the actions of these "religious" leaders, we can see that God will not hold them guiltless, because they have "carried" God's name in vain. Pedophile clergymen cause permanent psychological damage to innocent children. Equally appalling has been the willingness of the Church and other religious institutions to cover up these offensive practices, which has brought enormous damage to the respect for all clergy. Millions of dollars in law suits, prison sentences, psychiatric counseling, and even the decline in recruitment for the clergy, has been the result of these practices. The third commandment speaks directly to clerical offenses, such as sexual molestation and the conspiracy to conceal them, as unforgivable acts before God.

When a religious leader, whether Muslim, Christian, or Jewish, advocates suicide and murder in the name of God as an act of faith by its adherents, the Lord will not forgive them for these despicable acts of terror committed in His name. How can a Godly person of any faith applaud the suicide of those who attach bombs to themselves and detonate them killing dozens or hundreds, as they worship or go about daily activities riding a bus, eating in a restaurant, or shopping in a market place? Even more morally horrendous are those who teach children, and even the mentally challenged, to take their own lives in God's name to earn a reward in the next world.

Is this the God of justice and love in which all of humanity believes? Is this really what God has taught us, to cause excruciating pain in other human beings in His name? Often these bombing devices contain nuts and bolts, so that if the victims of the attack do survive, they will have irreparable damage to their organs and limbs that will cause them pain and suffering throughout the remainder of their lives.

Where is the outrage of the religious leaders of all faiths condemning such practices and teaching them to the next generation? I believe that by being silent about such tragic crimes committed in God's name, all of us are somewhat guilty of violating this third commandment, and none of us will be forgiven unless we stop these horrific suicides and murders, perpetuated by painful explosive devices being used as weapons in the name of God.

The Church officials, who ordered and approved the torture and murder of anusim in the name of God were "taking" the name of God in vain in violation of the third commandment. "For he that takes the name of the Lord thy God in vain shall not be held guiltless." Where is the recognition of that guilt?

Would God want the followers of such teachings to remain silent as these criminals bring such monstrous and violent behavior on others? Is it not altogether clear that the third commandment was given to mankind by God specifically to dissuade religious leaders and followers from performing evil acts in His name? Any act of evil committed in God's name violates this commandment, whereas any good performed in God's name honors the validity of this commandment.

I believe with all my soul that the message of the third commandment must be taught to all religious leaders of every faith that claim to believe in a God of justice. We still have the opportunity to fix things before it is too late, but if we remain silent and indifferent as religious people continue to "carry" God's name in a violent, immoral, and ungodly way, we will have violated the very essence and sanctity of the Ten Commandments which God gave to humanity to make this a good and decent world for all of His creatures.

Chapter Six

Tisha B'av, the Holiday for the B'nei Anusim

T ISHA B'AV, THE NINTH DAY OF THE HEBREW month of Av is considered to be the saddest day on the Jewish calendar. Traditional Jews fast for twenty-four hours, do not wear leather, sit on low benches or on the floor of the synagogue, and sometimes light small memorial candles in memory of the tragic events that occurred on that day in Jewish history. According to tradition, the first Holy Temple was destroyed by the Babylonians on the 9th day of Av in the year 586 B.C.E.

On that very same day, Tisha B'av, in the year 70 C.E. the second Holy Temple was destroyed by the Romans. In the year 1290 the Jews were expelled from England on the 9th of Av. In 1492 the Jews were expelled from Spain on Tisha B'av, the 9th day of Av. Although the last two events and others have occurred on this tragic day, they have usually been ignored in the observance of this holiday. The emphasis is usually placed on remembering the Holocaust and the destruction of the two Temples.

On Tisha B'Av we read the Book of Lamentations, called "Aicha", in Hebrew, which is one of the five Megillot or scrolls found in the Bible, along with Esther, Ruth, The Song of Songs, and Ecclesiastes. The Book of Aicha was authored by Jeremiah who witnessed the destruction of the Holy Temple by the Babylonians. In addition to the reading of Lamentations, *Kinot* or elegies written by different rabbis, authors, sages, and composers are read in synagogues.

These *Kinot* composed often in poetic form recall other tragic events in the history of the Jewish people. To a large extent, however, the expulsion of the Jews from Spain, receives little attention. I believe that this oversight, not giving full interest to the Spanish Inquisition and the anti-Semitic content of the Edict of Expulsion, misses an important opportunity to educate the Jewish world about that tragic period of Jewish history. It could also give positive attention to the return of the B'nei Anusim to Judaism today.

Many people are unaware of the fact that Christopher Columbus was supposed to sail for the New World on that day, but some say that he delayed disembarking because it was Tisha B'av. Since there is a possibility that Columbus himself was a converso this would not have been a good day to begin such an unpredictable journey. We also know that four of Columbus' crew were conversos of Jewish ancestry. Others say that Columbus had to delay the trip because all the ports of Spain were congested on that day with ships laden with departing Jews.

I believe that it is extremely important to educate our students, both young and old about this time in the history of the Jews of Spain. Many history books do not give adequate treatment of this historic event. I remember when I was growing up in Bridgeport, Connecticut that I was so proud because my Bar Mitzvah date, which occurred on the Sabbath of the Intermediate days of Sukkoth, coincided with the secular date of Columbus' birthday, namely October 12th.

I was so proud, because I had been taught that were it not for Columbus, none of us would be in America today, and furthermore, Queen Isabella and King Ferdinand were heroes, too, because they funded his voyage. We were never shown their Edict of Expulsion which accused Jews of being a horrible people who were destroying the Christian religion and the people of Spain.

In truth, Ferdinand and Isabella were evil monarchs on whose hands is the blood of tens of thousands of my Jewish ancestors, and they were directly responsible for the Expulsion of the Jews and the Inquisition. Since we are not taught this in school, wouldn't Tisha B'av be the perfect time to educate all of us about the facts and details of the horrors of the Inquisition, including the torture devices, the way anusim were forced to confess, the brutal way anusim were burned alive at the stake, and the total disregard for humanity, which the Church exhibited at that time.

This is very important for Jews and the world to learn, and Tisha B'av is the appropriate time to teach it. A few years ago, I was invited to address a group of high school history teachers of Austin High School in El Paso at a seminar, which was held prior to the beginning of the academic school year. My invitation came in order to inform the teachers about the Inquisition, which was not covered adequately in the students' text books, and also to speak about the return of the crypto-Jews, a unique happening in the city of El Paso.

The teachers were grateful for the information that I gave them and told me that it would be helpful to them in the semester that was about to begin. This learning experience proved to be valuable because someone took the time to care about updating new resources about a topic that had not received the attention it deserved.

I believe this shows how valuable it would be if we used the opportune time of Tisha B'av to educate our Jewish communities and others about the Expulsion, the Inquisition, and the return of the B'nei Anusim. In addition to the educational advantage of this decision, it would also lead to practical results. Tisha B'av is not the most observed of Jewish holidays because there are so many who are away from home and because it occurs when there is no religious school in session. It is not a joyful holiday, and attendance at many synagogues is sparse. Adding attention to the holiday by inviting a speaker, showing a film, having a dramatic presentation, or other special activities related to the Expulsion of the Jews from Spain might encourage more people to attend. Such programs giving information to people on the experience of the Spanish Jews and the return of the B'nei Anusim today are important for Jewish education.

Twenty years ago I began to introduce this activity to my Tisha B'av service. I invited a speaker from San Antonio, Richard Santos, who had just written a book about his discovery of having Jewish heritage. I advertised the event in the El Paso Times and invited people of all faiths who would like to learn more about the returning crypto-Jews of El Paso and Juarez. I explained the meaning of Tisha B'av, I also announced it in the Jewish Federation bulletin.

It was a huge success. Some 300 people attended that service. The previous year only fifteen had come. It was the largest number of people that had ever attended a Tisha B'av service in El Paso. The speaker was wonderful and related some very interesting and emotional details of the Jewish practices which were part of his Christian family's traditions while he was growing up in Mexico. He even told of the fact that when his grandmother baked tortillas in the oven, she took a piece of the corn dough and threw it into the oven. This is the Jewish practice which was performed when Jewish women baked "Challah", the special bread for Shabbat and festivals, and they would take a piece of the dough, or "challah" and offer it as a sacrifice, recalling the ancient tradition of Jewish history.

73

During the question and answer period that followed Mr. Santos' speech, many in attendance revealed their own personal stories of Jewish traditions that were practiced in their Catholic homes. Some people actually appeared to be making confessions that they knew that they had Jewish roots, but that they maintained their love for Jesus. Many people shed tears as they told their stories.

I was moved by the stories and the realization that over 300 people, both Jews and none Jews, had been motivated to attend this service and share their personal journeys. Among the speakers that we have had over the past decade include: Yaffa DeCosta who made Aliyah to Israel and works with the B'nei Anusim there and in other countries; Trudy Alexi of blessed memory who wrote the book, *The Mezuzah in Madonna's Foot,* her own personal crypto-Jewish story; Art Benveniste who is one of the officers of the Society for Crypto-Judaic Studies and whose story is very moving and informative; Sonya Loya, the founder and the director of the Bat Tziyon Learning Center of

Ruidoso, New Mexico;[6] Gabriela Bohm who produce the film, "The Longing: The Forgotten Jews of South America," which tells the story of B'nei Anusim in South America, who worked with Rabbi Jacques Cukiekorn, as they did their return, under very difficult circumstances. Rabbi Juan Mejia, another of my heroes and friends whose story I will tell later in this book, learned of his Jewish roots, converted to Judaism, attended the Jewish Theological Seminary of America and was ordained as a Conservative rabbi in 2009. He was one of the first of the B'nei Anusim in Colombia.

I felt so strongly about this idea to designate Tisha B'av as the time to recall the Spanish Expulsion, the Inquisition, and the return of the B'nei Anusim that I proposed it as a resolution at the United Synagogue for Conservative Judaism Biennial Convention in Cherry Hill, New Jersey, December 2009.

At that convention, my synagogue, Congregation B'nai Zion, had been selected to receive an award for the activities and programs, such as the annual Anusim conferences, that it had created to teach Jews and others about the B'nei Anusim. My wife Sharon, Dr. Jeffrey Weislow the president of the synagogue, and I made the trip to New Jersey to receive this award. Another facet of these conventions of the Conservative movement of Judaism is the presentation of resolutions, which are voted upon by the members who attend. These resolutions establish policies and procedures shape the direction and the future of the organization. In order to qualify, each resolution is presented to a committee, which then

6   I will tell her story in greater detail later in the book. She has been the spiritual inspiration of many B'nei Anusim who have returned to Judaism.

decides whether or not the resolution is worthy of being presented and receiving a vote.

As the date for the convention was drawing closer, I had not yet heard from the Resolution Committee whether or not my resolution to recognize the Spanish Jewish experience in T'isha B'av services would be presented. After arriving to the convention, I learned that there was some controversy about the content of my proposal. The committee could not decide what to do, and would allow me to present it, without their official approval or rejection. The day finally arrived, and I became a bit nervous about the responsibility that was on my shoulders regarding the presentation of what I believed to be a very important moment in my personal life and in the lives of the B'nei Anusim, whom I have taught for so many years.

When I was called, I stepped to the podium and spoke without a note in front of me. I spoke from the heart, with a few tears in my eyes, and told the assemblage of about 200 hundred delegates to this biennial convention, how passionate I was about the return of the B'nei Anusim, how vital I thought it was to teach our congregants of United Synagogue for Conservative Judaism on Tisha B'av about the history and impact of the Spanish Jewish experience on the Jewish world. This was an historic moment in our movement and in Judaism. When I finished my presentation, I received a standing ovation and the following resolution was passed unanimously:

Resolution welcoming B'nei Anusim to Judaism and memorializing the Spanish Inquisition as part of the Tisha B'av observances.

WHEREAS the fast day of Tisha B'av recalls the very Hebrew date upon which the Jews of Spain were expelled from their country in 1492; and

WHEREAS many Jews were forcibly converted to Christianity publicly then but continued to practice Judaism in secret; and

WHEREAS many of the descendants of those Jews, who are called B'nei Anusim, have returned formally to Judaism today, and many others are in the process of doing so;

THEREFORE BE IT RESOLVED that the United Synagogue of Conservative Judaism should cooperate with other arms of the Conservative movement to develop and disseminate appropriate educational materials welcoming the B'nei Anusim and memorializing the Spanish Inquisition as part of the Tisha B'av observances; and

BE IT FURTHER RESOLVED that the United Synagogue of Conservative Judaism encourages its affiliated congregations to use annual Tisha B'av observances as an occasion to inform their members of the return of the B'nei Anusim to Judaism, to welcome then into their congregations, and to educate their members about the tragedy of the Spanish Inquisition.

Rabbi Leon with family and friends at a night event
in front of Congregation B'nai Zion in El Paso.
Photo Ron D. Hart

Part Three

The Anusim and El Paso

Chapter Seven

B'nei Anusim Tour To Israel

I n March 2008 we organized a B'nei Anusim Tour to Israel, an eleven day trip where my intention was two-fold. First to encourage as many B'nei Anusim as possible to go and secondly to visit places and have speakers who were directly connected to the theme of crypto-Jews and the return to Judaism.

Of the twenty-nine people who went on the tour seventeen had B'nei Anusim backgrounds or connections. Through some fund-raising and a grant from the Jewish Federation of El Paso, I was able to provide scholarships to fund the entire cost or partial costs of some of the attendees.

Prior to the trip we had a meeting with those who were going on the tour and some of the special places that we would see in Israel. I also picked the time of the tour to take place during the festival of Purim because of the similarities between that holiday and the plight of the B'nei Anusim today.

The festival of Purim talks of a time in Jewish history when Haman, the prime-minister of Persia and the villain of the story, decided to exterminate the Jews because he did not approve of the way that they worshiped. This is similar to the thinking of the leaders of the Church, and the arch villain of the Jews, Torquemada, who wanted to rid Spain of Jews and Judaism. The other similarity is Esther, the heroine of the story, who hid her Jewish identity until the appropriate time and was responsible for saving her people and religion from the Persians who wanted to commit genocide against the Jews.

We arrived at Ben Gurion Airport and immediately said the prayer of "thanksgiving", which we call in Hebrew *shehecheyanu* and which says as follows, "Blessed are You O Lord, our God, Ruler of the Universe, Who has kept us in life, sustained us, and enabled us to reach this day." Many of the anusim shed tears as they had fulfilled the dream of coming to the Holy Land.

We met our guide Ronit Nachman, who was knowledgeable but not a particularly religious woman. Since she had little experience with B'nei Anusim, I told her about this history that was of special interest for us on this trip. Ironically, the year before I also had visited Israel, and on that visit our guide, Pilar Blanca, had a crypto-Jewish background. Pilar had been raised as a Catholic in Spain, visited Israel as a teenager, fell in love with the land, converted, and then learned of her crypto-Jewish ancestry. This was not the case with Ronit.

One of the highlights of our tour was the visit to the Doña Gracia House and Museum in Tiberias. The story of Doña Gracia is one of those secrets of Jewish history that very few Jews know about, even among Israelis. The story is well told in the wonderful book about her life by Andrée Aelion Brooks.[7] Doña Gracia was one of the great women heroes of Jewish history, who had the courage of the Biblical Esther, the heroine of Purim. Among

7   The Woman who Defied Kings: The Life and Times of Doña Gracia Nasi.

the families who were driven out of Spain in 1492 were Tsemach and Meir Benveniste who were brought to Portugal by their father to find refuge. Their Christian names were Francisco and Diogo Mendes. They were anusim, who had converted to Christianity publicly but still practiced Judaism secretly.

In 1510 a baby girl was born and baptized in Lisbon to the crypto-Jewish family named Miguis. She was given the Christian name Beatrice De Luna. Later on she was known as Gracia or Doña Gracia. Beatrice spent her childhood in her parents' elegant home with many servants and attended Sunday services in the Catholic church. Although she had seen candles being lighted on Friday nights in the cellar of the house, when she reached the age of thirteen, the age of Bat Mitzvah, her mother told Beatrice that she was a Jew. Her real name was Hannah Hanasi, and she was the daughter of anusim, who were expelled from Spain.

At eighteen she met her "*Beshert*", her "destined one", her chosen soul mate, the *chatan*, or groom, Francisco Mendez. He too, was from a B'nei Anusim family and his Hebrew name was Tsemach Benveniste. Francisco Mendez was wealthy. He owned the Mendez bank in Antwerp, Belgium and was one of the world's leading entrepreneurs who conducted business in the area of international trade with Far Eastern countries.

In spite of his wealth and the fact that he was openly practicing Christianity, Francisco always remained true to his roots. He remembered that Judaism had begun with a Jew by choice, respectfully honored with the title *Avraham Avinu*, "Abraham, our father".

The traditions of the crypto-Jews have been the link in the chain that goes back to Abraham, Sarah, Moses, and Tziporah. Teaching this to Jewish children at this time was quite dangerous and very difficult. Just as Sabbath and festival customs had to be hidden, so, too, teaching one's children Hebrew, Torah, or Talmud were risky responsibilities.

Therefore, Jewish education was taught in very secretive ways. Tsemach and Hannah were blessed with a daughter, Reyna, who was their pride and happiness. Despite the danger of the time in which they lived they ensured that Reyna would carry on Jewish traditions, secretly, from generation to generation.

With more imminent threats coming from the horrors of the Inquisition, at the same time the family wealth grew astronomically due to the expanding Far East trade in spices, especially black pepper. The family moved first to London and then to Antwerp in 1536.

On two occasions Doña Gracia was able to have Diogo released from prison after he had been arrested on false charges. Unfortunately at that time, after the second release from prison, Tsemach passed away leaving Doña Gracia a very wealthy widow who had to raise her daughter without a father.

As the Inquisition continued to spread throughout Portugal and massive arrests and forced conversions were taking place against the Jews, Doña Gracia saw the need to save her people from extermination. After Diogo died in 1542, Doña Gracia moved to Italy where she was accused of Judaizing and arrested by the Inquisition. But somehow, with her courage, her ingenuity, her faith, and yes, her enormous wealth, she managed to overcome even that adversity.

After escaping the Inquisition, she moved to the Ottoman, which was welcoming Jews. With the help of her nephew Joseph and her tenacity and charm, Doña Gracia became the first Zionist, some 400 years before Theodore Herzl, the founder of political Zionism. She convinced the Sultan of the Ottoman Empire to grant her the deed to the city of Tiberias, as a sanctuary for Sephardic Jews including people of crypto-Jewish background.

Doña Gracia was the first woman Zionist in history. Today in the beautiful city of Tiberias near the Sea of Galilee, one can visit the hotel and museum of Doña Gracia. It is an important place to visit if you really want to learn about crypto-Jews and the true story of this heroine and Zionist.

First we were given a lecture by one of the docents of the museum, a former crypto-Jew herself named Irena, who told us of her personal story and of the life and biography of Doña Gracia. After the inspiring lecture, we took a tour of the museum and saw some of the possessions that had been part of Doña Gracia's life.

We then were given a short piano recital by another woman on the staff of the museum. After her few piano selections she brought our group to a dressing room where there were about one hundred costumes depicting the time in which Doña Gracia lived. Most of us dressed in costumes of the medieval life of the crypto-Jews of Portugal, and the docent gave a brief presentation suggesting the roles we would be playing at that time. I was dressed as a judge, which might have been one of the roles of the rabbi in the community in that era.

Before we left the museum we took a group picture in front of the hotel. We hugged Irena and invited her to visit us. So many people on the tour told me that this was the highlight of the entire trip. When we returned to the bus, the guide Ronit told me that she had been a guide for many years and had never heard of the Doña Gracia museum. Now that she visited it with us, she would include it in the new tours that she would lead. She actually thanked me for taking her to the museum.

84

Another stop on our B'nei Anusim tour, which reflected the theme of our trip was the visit to Safed, the home of Kabbalah or Jewish mysticism. One of the early leaders of Kabbalah was Moshe de Leon, a thirteenth century Sephardic rabbi who gave the classic work, *The Zohar: the Book of Splendor*, to the world. He is part of my genealogy, I believe.

We visited a number of Sephardic synagogues in Safed, and when the *Shammas*, opened the ark of the Joseph Caro synagogue, I led the B'nei Anusim in chanting the prayer "*Vayihee Binsoa Ha'Aron*", which is what is said at services when we take out the Torah. He allowed us to come forward and kiss the Torah, a great honor for every Jew. For those of us on the trip, it was an unbelievable privilege to kiss the Torah in the Safed synagogue named for one of the greatest Sephardic rabbis in history, Joseph Caro, the author of the *Shulchan Aruch*, the compendium of Jewish law.

We arrived in Jerusalem on a Friday evening and before we came to the Western Wall, the holiest sight for the Jewish people, we stopped the bus, we made a Kiddush over the wine and we said the *Sheheceyanu* prayer again, the same blessing we invoked when we landed in Israel.

But now, we were about to enter Jerusalem, Yerushaly-im, the "City of Peace", Jerusalem of "gold", and so in addition to the prayer over the wine and the prayer of thanksgiving I also offered a special prayer for the descendants of the anusim who were here, as witness to the continuity of the Jewish people.

I told our group that our being here today resurrects the souls of the anusim who were forced to give up their Judaism 500 years ago but never really extinguished the candle of Judaism. On eve of Sabbath, here in Jerusalem, we were symbolically rekindling those flames of hope, prayer, and the future.

85

I stood by Hannah, a six month old baby, who was on her tour with her parents Gilbert and Alia. The mother, Alia, had just learned that she was a B'nei Anusim and was starting her process of return. I blessed Hannah with the Priestly Benediction, "May the Lord Bless you and Keep You, May God's face shine upon you and be gracious unto you. May God's Face Turn to You and Grant You Shalom and Let Us all Say Amen." I think that I even noticed a tear welling up in Ronit's eyes when I offered that prayer for Hannah.

After that emotional pause in our journey, we went directly to the Western Wall. The women went to their side and the men walked to the men's side of the division or *micheetza* between the genders.

After about twenty minutes in which each person touched the Wall, offered a prayer, and perhaps even wrote a note and placed it in the Wall, we gathered together on the steps located past the plaza of the Wall. I led Kabbalat Shabbat services, the prayers, which are made of Psalms welcoming the Sabbath into each Jewish community throughout the world.

This part of the Friday evening Jewish worship service was actually introduced to our liturgy by the Kabbalists of Safed. They used to dress in white clothes and would personally invite and welcome the Sabbath Queen, the Sabbath Bride into their community. I told the group before beginning the service that the first time I came to Jerusalem in 1962, I was spending the year between high school graduation and college in Israel. I was seventeen-years-old at the time, and I wasn't aware that as a Jew I was not permitted to come to the Western Wall. We called it "The Wailing Wall" then. Old Jerusalem had been under Jordanian control since 1948, and we were supposed to have access to our Jewish Holy places, but it simply didn't happen. It was a very sad realization for me that I will never forget.

However, the second time I came to Jerusalem was six years later in 1968 on my honeymoon. This was one year after the Six Day War of June 1967, when through a miraculous victory, Israel had reunified Jerusalem. With pride and humility my wife Sharon and I came to our respective sides of the Wall. Without any shame, I cried loudly as I kissed the stones that had been prohibited to me just six years before. I shared my emotion and once again shed tears as I told the group how fortunate we are today that we have been able with God's help to come to this most Holy place. How blessed our children are who have never been rejected from the Wall, as I was as a teenager.

Finally, I said how truly blessed we are together with the B'nei Anusim that by our mere presence at the Western Wall on Erev Shabbat, this evening of the Sabbath, we are proclaiming to the world in song and prayer that our ancestors are alive. The Inquisition did not take away their souls, which are intertwined with our souls, and they will return someday, and we will pray together as we do at this moment with song and praise and gratitude to you, O God.

Then, I began the service with the opening words of Psalm 95, *L'chu N'raninah La'adonye, Nariah Litzur, Yee-haynu,* "O come Let us Sing Unto the Lord, My Rock In Whom There is No Unrighteousness." I will never forget that moment and how privileged and yet how humbled I was at the presence of all the B'nei Anusim facing the Wall and offering those prayers. After the service, we hugged and wished each other "Shabbat Shalom" and returned to our hotel for the lighting of the Shabbat candles and a delicious traditional Shabbat dinner.

The next morning we went to the Great Synagogue, which was across the street from our hotel. We listened to the harmonious male choir and guest Cantor Chaim Stern chant the service with true "Kavanah", which means "directed devotion" and spirit. I had arranged for Jack Zeller, who at that time was the President of Kulanu and was living in Jerusalem, to meet us at the service, have lunch with us at the hotel, and then to talk to us about all the work that Kulanu does to help Jewish communities in the most remote parts of the world, including the B'nei Anusim.

Jack gave us an interesting update on Jewish communities in Africa, the Abudaya and Lemba tribes, what was happening in other countries, the Ethiopians who have come to Israel, and about the crypto-Jews in the United States, South America, and Europe. Jack Zeller's participation was another important moment on our B'nei Anusim journey.

A few days later we went to "Masada", the last stronghold of the Jews in the struggle against the Roman conquest of Israel and the destruction of the second Holy Temple in the year 70 C.E. According to the traditional story of Masada as recorded by the historian of that time Josephus Flavius and substantiated by the respected Israeli archeologist Yigal Yadin, the Jews who went to Masada were "Zealots". They held out for three years against the Romans. At Masada we can find a synagogue, a Mikvah, storehouses for food, and other indications that the people wanted to live there long term.

According to Josephus, when the Zealots learned that the Romans were about to overtake them they decided under the leadership of Eliezer ben Yair to kill the women and children and then to commit suicide as an act of courage and defiance against the Romans. Rather than subject the women and children to certain torture, rape, slavery and other evils, the men decided to avoid these horrific acts by dying as martyrs rather than as victims.

The very first time that I was at Masada, was in 1962 as a teenager when I spent a year in Israel on a program called *Hamachon L'Madrichei Chutz La'Aretz*, which in English translates as "The Institute for Youth Leaders From Abroad," representing nineteen different countries and several foreign languages. As part of that educational program to teach us about Israel, we were taken to some of the most important historical sites, including Masada.

I will never forget that visit. We climbed up the mountain via the "snake" trail, and it took us about two hours. When we finally made it to the top, we were exhausted, thirsty, covered with sweat. Then, we heard the noise of people running up the mountain, as we looked down we saw a group of Israeli paratroopers running up the mountain, each carrying a forty pound backpack.

We learned from our guide that we were witnessing something very special, the inauguration of a group of Israeli militia who were being sworn in as members of the *"Tzamchaneem"*, the "paratroopers", which is considered Israel's elite branch of the Israel Defense Forces, and one of the best military units in the world. After months of training, the *Tzamchaneem* would run up the trail leading to Masada, and then when they arrived at the top, they were given their new credentials as official members of the Israeli paratroopers.

As they accepted this special honor, the troop would pledge together these words, *Matzada Lo Tipol Shayneet* which means, "Masada Shall Never Fall Again". It really was a magnificent moment that I will always remember. Later that evening, I had a discussion with my roommate, Silvio from Rome, Italy, whose Hebrew name was Shalom.

I told him that while I was impressed with Masada I really had great difficulty in understanding and accepting the historical account given by Josephus Flavius. I couldn't understand why the Zealots did not go down fighting, even the women and children. What is so courageous about committing suicide, which is forbidden in Judaism.

There are only two other cases of Jews committing suicide rather than fall to the enemy that I recall. The Jews of York in the eleventh century during the Crusades, and the ninety-three women of the Beit Ya'akov Yeshiva during the Holocaust who killed themselves rather than be raped by the Nazis.

But Masada requires even more scrutiny because in this case reportedly Jewish men actually killed the women and children. This is not suicide, it's actually pre-meditated murder, forbidden by the Torah. I cannot understand this as a courageous act whatsoever. I don't believe it happened this way. And so I did further research on Josephus. Could he have had an ulterior motive in his report and did he actually witness the killings?

Answering the second question first, I learned that Josephus was not at Masada when the killings took place. He came there later and heard the report from two women, who supposedly had survived the incident, and they gave their version of what happened. How do we know that their testimony is correct? How do we know that there really were such witnesses? How do we know that they were not trying to cover up their own actions, which might have not been admirable? How do we know that they happened to survive because they were in alliance with the Romans?

In answer to the first question, I also discovered that there were mixed reviews concerning Josephus' reliability as a historian and as one loyal to the Jewish people. There were suggestions that at times Josephus was loyal to the Jews and other times that he was loyal to the Romans, and sometimes a little bit of both. For example, in another incident when Josephus was a general in the community near Yotfata in the Galilee, it is reported that Josephus' brigade was in a cave and found themselves surrounded by a large Roman legion.

When it was evident to Josephus that his unit was going to fall, he convinced them to take their own lives rather than give the enemy the satisfaction of a military victory. Every one but Josephus did just that, and then he walked away alive and safe. Is it possible that Josephus made up the account of a mass murder/suicide pact at Masada in order to justify his own cowardice and betrayal as a general in Yotfata?

91

I personally believe that the Zealots went down fighting. That's it. End of story. They lived as courageous Jews and died as courageous Jews. I believe that Josephus got the story wrong. Since he was the only historian to write the account of that event, which he did not personally witness, I believe that his account can be open to question. Then, some will respond, but what about the great archaeological expert on Masada, Professor Yigal Yadin, of blessed memory, whose findings gave credibility to Josephus' narrative? I can only answer that Yadin's work was done within the context of the Josephus history, and that might have influenced his interpretation of the archaeological findings.

After reading Yadin's book and the report of Josephus, and comparing it to my theory that the Masada defenders went down fighting, I see no inconsistency in either possibility. The evidence of Yadin proves that the Zealots were there, that they had food stored there, that there was a mikvah, a synagogue, and that they died there. It does not prove how they died. Trude Weiss Rosemarin and others have also proposed alternative interpretations of the Masada story.

My thinking about Masada is further substantiated by the story of the crypto-Jews. Like the Zealots of Masada they could have committed suicide rather than convert to Christianity, but they didn't. They went through torture, watching family and friends murdered and burnt alive, and yet they continued to practice their Judaism secretly for generation after generation.

And now 500 years later, because of their courage, their descendants, the B'nei Anusim, are returning. In other words their courage and thirst for life quenched the fires of the Inquisition and their return today is the testimony to their bravery and desire to survive. They never killed themselves or their children or family members. They stayed alive, and they are alive.

I do believe that the victims of Masada were heroes and martyrs because they fought to the end and went down fighting, as has always been the way of courage for Jews. As a Texas rabbi today, I "remember the Alamo" in which Davy Crockett and Jim Bowie and a community of courageous men and women went down fighting the Mexicans. Had they committed suicide and killed women and children first, what would there be to remember?

The rallying cry of the Israeli paratroopers that "Masada Shall Never Fall Again" is a courageous affirmation if it is said believing that our ancestors went down fighting. In contrast, if they gave up and killed women and children before committing suicide, how could that be a rallying cry for the strongest and best trained branch of Israel's Defense Forces?

I am not sure that Ronit Nachman agreed with my version of the story, but I am sure that she will think about it, and I am also positive that the B'nei Anusim who came with me to Masada understood that I could not be silent when their history is so filled with courage and the will to survive under any circumstance.

When we arrived in Tel Aviv, we visited the Diaspora Museum, which is in Ramat Aviv, part of Tel Aviv University. It was a important place to visit for it documents the genealogy and history of the Jewish people with records, archeology, recreations, art work, writings, and computer technology. The section that dealt with the Spanish Inquisition gave our B'nei Anusim clear evidence of the horrific events that the Jews suffered during that awful time and confirmed the reality that indeed we are seeing the rebirth of the descendants of that tragic era.

In the historical section, which dates events chronologically, it clearly states that it was the Sephardic Kabbalist, my great ancestor, Moshe de Leon who authored the Zohar. As another episode of the trip, related to the museum visit and which I want to share, is an experience that I had on Purim in Jerusalem.

We actually observed Purim with the reading of the Megillat Esther, the Scroll of Esther at a synagogue at a small *moshav* near Tiberias. We were accepted and treated well by the Rabbi, but unfortunately the women were not so comfortable in the women's section without any books to follow the service or the reading of the Megillah.

In Israel Purim fell on Thursday night, but there is a tradition that in a walled in city, like Jerusalem, that the holiday is extended through Saturday night. After leaving

Tiberias we came to Jerusalem for Shabbat and immediately thereafter on Saturday night, when Shabbat ended, we would go back to the city for the continuation of Purim celebrations. We were on Ben Yehudah Street and young people were in costume, setting off fire crackers and having fun.

My wife and I and another couple went into a jewelry and religious goods store to buy gifts for family members. Suddenly two Americans dressed in religious white robes came into the store and seemed to be quite friendly. One of them was wearing the "Rabbi Nachman" yarmulke which is made up of the first letters of Reb Nachman's name. I politely asked one of the men who said that he was from Florida and studying at a Yeshiva to explain the meaning to me. He did so with a little humor and things were going well.

He then asked me if I knew anything about Kabbalah. I said to him in a nice way that not only did I study Kabbalah but that my great-great grandfather was Moshe de Leon, the author of the Zohar. All of a sudden his mood changed to anger. "What do you mean Moshe de Leon wrote the Zohar!" He shouted at me, "It was Shimon Bar Yochai!"

Again, I responded politely, "You know, there are differences of opinion on the subject. In fact, when we were in the Diaspora Museum it clearly affirmed that the author was Moshe de Leon." At that point, the religious Floridian lost it. He slapped me across the face and swore at me over and over again in English and Hebrew and said that I was an "Epicoros," which is a Jewish term implying "non-believer".

I didn't know what to do, but rather than hit or grab the man and risk damaging the store's delicate merchandise, or getting into a fist fight, I decided to respond quietly,

94

You know, young man, you have no idea who I am, what I do or why I am in Israel. Your violent actions should make you ashamed, ashamed that you wear the kippah of Reb Nachman, ashamed that you have embarrassed Judaism and your Yeshivah, and ashamed because it is clear from your violence that you haven't learned anything of value from your Yeshivah. What would your teachers say to you if they saw what you did to another Jew simply because he politely disagreed with your point of view. Isn't that what Talmudic study is all about?

Unfortunately my words, which were intended to calm the student, only irritated him further and he continued to curse and call me names. He even tried to attack me.

Finally, the store owner and another friend actually removed him from the store. The store owner then apologized to me, and I responded, "You don't owe me an apology, but the sacred objects and scrolls in your shop have been blasphemed by this man, who thinks that he is religious. What a *shanda!* I bring B'nei Anusim to Israel, and this man slapped me for having a different point of view.

My thought was that is exactly the same mentality that led to the Crusades and the Inquisition! I will never forget that slap. To me it represents the brainwashing to which a person can be exposed when he or she does not have a foundation in understanding the sacred.

I rail against the Kabbalistic teachers of Madonna and other superstars. Madonna is not even Jewish and in my opinion a rabbi should not be teaching her. Kabbalah shops in Beverly Hills, "holy water" sold at her concerts, amulets and red strings that are being sold to ward off evil, makes Judaism into "voodoo". It has resulted in Hollywood Kabbalah becoming a big business. I was in Los Angeles last year and heard a radio commercial inviting people of all faiths to come to a Kabbalah Center to learn the mysteries of Kabbalah.

96

The Torah warns us against witchcraft, false prophets, sorcery, etc because these are pagan practices, which are the antithesis of Torah. Jewish tradition teaches us that it is actually dangerous for one's psychological well-being to study Kabbalah until one is familiar with the teachings of Judaism and the Torah, and, in addition, a person should not engage in the study of Kabbalah until he is at least forty years old.

When people make Kabbalah an entrepreneurial venture or fad and make it into a money maker, then they demean the Torah. The slap that I received on that Purim in Jerusalem, was the slap of ignorance, hypocrisy, hatred and evil, which even Judaism can become.

It is clear to me that this was the exact mindset that led religious Christians to use torture devices and even worse, to burn people alive, who simply believed differently than they did. It might start with a slap, but who knows where that can lead? In spite of that ugly and painful experience that I had in the store, it was very special to experience Purim with B'nei Anusim, both at the *Moshav* and in Jerusalem.

One of the highlights of our visit to Tel Aviv, which occurred near the end of our tour, was the opportunity to meet and hear the message of Rabbi Nissan ben Avraham. Ever since I saw the video of Yitzhak Navon, which I mentioned before, Rabbi Nissan has been one of my heroes. Rabbi Nissan truly encompasses what B'nei Anusim represent to the world Jewish community. When a person, such as Rabbi Nissan, learns about his Jewish ancestry, even though he is living as a Catholic, and decides to explore his Jewish roots and return to Judaism, it helps me to focus on the fact that my involvement with the B'nei Anusim is valuable.

97

The former Nicholas Aguilo could have done research about Judaism and that would have sufficed, but that wasn't enough for him. There was something in his soul, his *neshamah,* as we say in Hebrew, which drove him to return to that religion, which was stolen from his family when his ancestors were forced to convert in 1391.

Nicholas did not simply return, he did a full conversion in Israel. He then continued to study beyond his conversion. He continued further with studies on an even higher level and ultimately by virtue of his scholarship and dedication to his Jewish education, earned the distinction to be ordained as a Rabbi by the chief Rabbinate of Israel.

He then wrote, *Els Anussim* about the halachic, or Jewish legal, requirements for the B'nei Anusim to return to Judaism. To me, Rabbi Nissan is important because he is living proof that although the Spanish Crown and the Catholic Church succeeded in their goal of driving the Jews out of Spain, they could not destroy Judaism. On the contrary, it has inspired descendants of its victims to rise up, return, and become teachers of Judaism. I view Rabbi

Nissan as a vehicle of God, to lead the return that is beginning to happen. The Church did not eradicate the Aguilo Jewish family of Palma, Majorca, rather it created a new instructor of Judaism to emerge 500 years later, who would devote his life to studying, practicing, and teaching those very traditions, customs, laws, values, and principles of Judaism, which the Church attempted to eliminate.

Rabbi Nissan ben Avraham carries the banner of God proudly, which the Third Commandment obligates all of us to do, in spite of the Church that defiled that banner when it arrested, tortured, killed and expelled Rabbi Nissan's ancestors. The Church failed because it desecrated the commandment and the word of God, and it desecrated it with pride and defiance. How sad and how frightening it is that so many "religious" Christians could do so much evil in God's name. But there stands, Rabbi Nissan, one Jew, one rabbi, one of the B'nei Anusim. His return to Judaism and ordination as a rabbi speaks louder than an entire Inquisition. It shouts out for all to hear, "*Am Yisrael Chai!*", "the People of Israel Lives".

Rabbi Nissan is the living representative of the souls that were hovering about the Plaza de Rossi in Lisbon when I offered the memorial prayer for them. He brings their souls alive for you and for me and for all people who love God and who want people of God to act godly. And so when I was able to arrange for Rabbi Nissan to come to Tel Aviv from his home in Shilo where he teaches and is a *Sofeir*, a scribe who writes Torahs and other Holy scrolls for *Mezuzot* and tefillin, it was very special for me, and I knew that he would inspire the entire tour group.

When I met Rabbi Nissan for the first time, I recognized him immediately. I first shook his hand and then gave him a hug. I don't think that Rabbi Nissan understood how much I idolized and loved him, even though I had never met him before. Rabbi Nissan had dinner with us and after the meal we chanted the *Birkat HaMazon*, the "Grace After Meals" together.

Then, Rabbi Nissan began to talk about his life in Majorca. He spoke about his Catholic upbringing and how he discovered his Jewish roots and the journey that he took to return fully to those roots. He is the only one in his family that took this path, which tells us about the very special qualities that Rabbi Nissan possesses. He also showed us the family tree that his brother had put together tracing 500 years of their family. The talk of Rabbi Nissan was inspiring, and to me it was one of the special moments of my life. I know that he stands as an example and a role model for those who will follow and will return. The B'nei Anusim trip to Israel was, I believe, the beginning of the return of many crypto-Jews to visit and also to make Aliyah to Israel.

Rabbi Leon speaking at the Anusim Conference 2016
Photo Ron D. Hart

Chapter Eight
The Anusim Center and Anusim Conferences

O N AUGUST 10TH, 2014 A DREAM OF MINE
came true: the dedication of the Anusim Center
of El Paso. Several years ago, Sonya Loya, Rabbi Juan Mejia, and I discussed the possibility of estab-
lishing a central location to offer information, research
and study regarding the B'nei Anusim. In the fall of 2013,
I invited a group of local members of the El Paso Jewish community to help me establish such a center. The
founding members of the Anusim Center came from a
variety of backgrounds. Some had crypto-Jewish roots,
who had formally returned to Judaism. One was an individual of Ashkenazi origin whose grandparents had
perished in Auschwitz. Some board members had come
to Israel with me on the Anusim tour, and others had
observed their B'nai Mitzvah at our synagogue.

The board met almost every week for several months,
creating a mission statement, exploring a location for our
center, formulating our goals and developing our plans.
The original location of the Anusim Center occupies the
former home of the El Paso Holocaust Museum on the
campus of the Jewish Community Center of El Paso. Unfortunately, a fire had destroyed many of the artifacts in
that museum and its board of directors decided to move
that museum to downtown El Paso. A portion of that edifice housed the Jewish Family and Children's Services

of El Paso, but the part that had been the home of the Holocaust Museum had been empty for many years. The El Paso Jewish Academy purchased that land and generously allowed the Anusim Center to lease that part of the building rent-free, a generous gesture that we really appreciate.

The legal name is the Sephardic Anusim Cultural Heritage Resource Center, commonly know as The Anusim Center of El Paso. The mission statement of the Center adapted by its board of directors is as follows: "The Anusim Center shall disseminate information of the historical effects of the Spanish Inquisition on Sephardic Jewry and provide this education to the public and to the descendants of those who were forcibly converted or expelled from the Iberian Peninsula and to make available a path for those who desire a return to their Jewish ancestral heritage."

The dedication ceremony was a huge success. Representatives of many organizations came to show their support. A proclamation was read from Mayor Oscar Leeser naming this occasion as "The Day of Dedication of the Anusim Center of El Paso." My colleague, Rabbi Larry Bach offered greetings from his congregation, Temple Mt. Sinai of El Paso. Rabbi Larry Karol of Temple Beth El, Las Cruces, New Mexico offered a benediction. Cesar Carrasco, the President of our synagogue, Congregation B'nai Zion, offered words of support.

In addition dignitaries from the Jewish Federation, the El Paso Holocaust Museum, the Hispanic Chamber of Commerce, the Food Bank of El Paso, and the El Paso Jewish Academy expressed words of encouragement. An important letter expressing a desire to work together with the B'nei Anusim came from Professor Avraham Gross the director of the Institute for Sefardi Anousim Studies of the Netanya Academic College of Israel. Joe Lovett, director of the film, "Children of the Inquisition" also wrote an inspiring letter of congratulations. The event was covered by local television and media and was also reported in a number of international periodicals. This was indeed was a marvelous time of rejoicing, celebration, and dedication.

103

The Anusim Center offers the world a place where the history, culture, and influence of the B'nei Anusim and crypto-Jews is presented through educational programs, musical presentations, lectures, films, food, poetry, art, dance, photo exhibits, conferences, guest speakers, genealogical research. Those who want to learn and experience the world of the anusim now have a place where informational resources are available. Those of crypto-Jewish background will be able to take courses on their history, on Judaism, and even will be afforded the opportunity to return formally to their Jewish heritage which was forcibly stolen from them at the time of the Spanish Inquisition.

Since the founding of the Anusim Center, many displays, musical concerts, speakers, lecturers, a coffee house, and even a marriage took place. On the day of dedication an exhibit of photographs, stories, and biographies of crypto-Jews of the Southwest including many from El Paso was on display at the Anusim Center.

Gloria Golden, a photographer and author who resides in New York had come to the Southwest several years ago and had written the book, "Remnants of Crypto-Jews among Hispanic Americans". Gloria had enlarged each of her photographs along with the stories and lectured on the subject for several years. As she prepared to retire, she and I were in contact, and she generously donated her exhibit to our center.

In addition, a trailer of Joe Lovett's film was shown and a good part of it included an interview with me and with several B'nei Anusim from my community. One of the recent guest speakers was Professor Asher Mattathias of St. John's University who spoke on the relationship of the Holocaust to the Spanish Inquisition. The Anusim Center has a wonderful logo, which was created by one of our founders and board member, photographer Donald Scharf. Don photographed an image of Jacob's ladder at sunset in Santa Fe, New Mexico.

This moving photograph is similar to the original ladder of Jacob with the anusim ascending and descending the Divine ladder going up to God, as they continue their arduous journey of return. As we expand the work of our center, we will offer genealogical research and orientation for those wishing to explore their genetic identity through DNA. The Anusim Center is the only place I know where those who decide to return to their Jewish roots have an infrastructure to support them.

In the three decades that I have devoted to teaching and advising B'nei Anusim, between sixty and seventy families have made their return. With the establishment of the Anusim Center, I expect those figures to expand. Our goal is not to proselytize but rather to welcome and offer understanding to those who have discovered their Jewish roots.

The people are the most positive and gratifying aspect of the Anusim Center, including the Board of Directors, who are individuals that care deeply and are filled with dedication and passion. It is a privilege to be the Director of such an outstanding center, which displays such character and commitment. Guests, including speakers who enter our doors marvel at the very positive, passionate and spiritual mood of those who are members and participants in our programs. It is truly a place of Godliness, hope, mission and spirituality.

105

The Anusim Conferences

Now in the second decade, the Anusim conferences have been organized to inform, educate, publicize, and welcome those interested in the phenomenon of the B'nei Anusim returning to Judaism. Sonya Loya the founder and director of the Bat Tziyon Learning Center in Ruidoso, New Mexico was the one person most responsible for the conference and its success. She organized and co-ordinated the first conference which took place in Ruidoso. I first learned of Sonya through a newspaper article which was sent to me by a congregant, who has a business in Ruidoso.

At that time Sonya was conducting Sabbath services at the learning center along with study sessions. Those who attended were learning Hebrew, Torah, and other related subjects about Judaism. Sonya herself learned of her Jewish roots when she was about thirty years old. I came in touch with Sonya when one of my congregants visited her shop and suggested that Sonya call me. Soon thereafter we began our relationship and started to work together to help bring the descendants of crypto-Jews back to Judaism. In fact, Sonya did her return after studying with me for about a year.

Two years later Sonya's daughter Rachel also did her return with me after a year of study. Rachel's return represented to me further proof that the phenomenon of crypto-Jewish influence is an ongoing reality, which will continue to grow from one generation to the next. Thanks to Sonya's initiative and passion, the Anusim conferences have continued from the first one in Ruidoso in 2003, the one in Israel in 2008, and the rest that have been in El Paso at Congregation B'nai Zion. These inspirational conferences have attracted visitors and speakers from the four corners of the world.

106

One of the early speakers was Stanley Hordes, a pioneer in crypto-Jewish studies, whose book *To the End of the Earth: a History of the Crypto-Jews of New Mexico* is recognized as a fundamental book in the study of the B'nei Anusim of New Mexico. Another speaker was Prof. Seth Kunin, Deputy Vice-Chancellor, International at Curtin University, Perth, Australia. One of the most respected authorities on the secret Jews of Spain, Prof. David Gitlitz, was the keynote speaker in 2014 and his book, *Secrecy and Deceit: the Religion of Crypto-Jews* is the classic reference book among experts on this subject. In another book, *A Drizzle of Honey: the Life and Recipes of Spain's Secret Jews*, Prof. Gitlitz gives recipes and stories of crypto-Jews who perished in the Inquisition but whose recipes survived. In the 2014 conference, Mario Ochoa, a chef and B'nei Anusim, catered a Shabbat meal using recipes from this book.

Other speakers over the years have included:

- Corinne Joy Brown, editor of *HaLapid,* a publication of the Society for Crypto-Judaic Studies, and author of the novel *Hidden Star* on crypto-Jewish life, has been a speaker on two occasions.
- Rabbi Peter Tarlow has spoken at several conferences. He is the Director of the Center for Latino-Jewish Relations and Crypto-Jewish Studies at Texas A&M University and is currently the Chairperson of the Texas Holocaust and Genocide Commission.
- Rabbi Juan Mejia, the first B'nei Anusim to be ordained as a rabbi by the Jewish Theological Seminary of America.
- Rabbi Nissan ben Avraham of Shilo, Israel, who was ordained by the chief Rabbinate of Israel after living as a crypto-Jew in Majorca.
- Rabbi Danny Mehlman, spiritual leader of Temple Ner Tamid, Downey, California, and one who travels to Mexico and South America regularly facilitating the return of B'nei Anusim to their roots.
- Prof. Avraham Gross, Director of the Institute for Sephardi and Anousim Studies at Netanya Academic College, Israel, was the keynote speaker in 2015.

In addition to these informative speakers, the Anusim conferences have presented concerts of Judeo-Spanish music by the Sephardic singer Vanessa Paloma and Cantor Marc Phillipe, as well as displaying the art work of people of anusim descent.

These conferences are held over a Shabbat week-end with religious services and words of Torah as an important component of the experience. Over 1500 attendees have learned, discussed, and offered their own stories regarding the crypto-Jewish experience.

One of the highlights have been the wedding ceremonies of couples with B'nei Anusim backgrounds. Often the conference coincides with the Jewish holiday of Tu B'av, which is an occasion for couples to express their love for each other.

Peter Svarzbein, an El Paso city councilman, performance artist and activist, often provides a kosher taco truck with the theme, "*Conversos y Tacos*" for the Saturday night dinner for the conference, He includes a printed menu, which gives the basic history of crypto-Jews, as well as a video program with photographs and stories of personal journeys of those who have returned to their Jewish roots.

Chapter Nine

Israel Television Comes To El Paso
To Cover the B'nei Anusim

DURING THE FESTIVAL OF CHANUKAH 2006, Israel television, Channel One, came to El Paso to cover the activities of the B'nei Anusim in El Paso, and specifically at Congregation B'nai Zion.

The Story of Chanukah

There is a direct connection between the meaning of Chanukah and the return of the B'nei Anusim. Chanukah commemorates the miraculous victory of the Maccabees over the Syrian Hellenistic nation which invaded Israel in 175 B.C.E. The conquest of Israel was not the only goal of the invasion, but the end of Judaism was also part of the plan.

For that reason, the Syrian general Antiochus, desecrated the Holy Temple, by smearing it with pig's blood and placing a large idol of himself in the central part of the sanctuary. The general called himself Antiochus Epiphanies, which implied that he was a god. He threatened Jews by death if they didn't worship him. There is a parallel with the Spanish experience. In the case of Chanukah, conversion to Hellenism was the goal, and in Spain it was conversion to Catholicism.

At the time of Chanukah, the Priest of the Holy Temple was Mattathias who challenged the threats of Antiochus. He ordered the Jews to remain steadfast in their faith in *Adonye* and also threatened Jews who would become pagans. Mattathias had five sons who led a revolution against the invading Syrian nation. The leader of the sons was Judah who was called "Maccabee", which means "hammer" in Hebrew, implying that Judah was capable of defeating his adversaries. It also stands for the acronym in Hebrew made of four Hebrew letters, " " which stands for the phrase, *Mi Kamocha Ba-Eilim Adonye*, which means, "Who is like unto You, O Lord, among the gods (of the heathens)". After three years, the Maccabees successfully drove out the Syrians and proclaimed victory. They rededicated the Holy Temple after cleansing it and refurnishing it with the Jewish religious objects.

Chanukah means "dedication", and it refers to the re-dedication of the Holy Temple at that time almost 2200 years ago. The Jews refused to give up Judaism during that time, and this is true of the B'nei Anusim, who also maintained their Jewish traditions during the Spanish Inquisition.

After the Syrian god was removed from the Holy Temple, it was time to kindle the *Ner Tamid*, or "Eternal Light", which is a symbol of God's presence to this very day in synagogues throughout the world. Unfortunately there was only enough Kosher oil found to last one day, and it would take four days to reach the nearest place to replenish the oil and four days back. The question was whether or not to light the *Ner Tamid* anyway. After all, had the light gone out, it would not be "eternal" and perhaps would indicate that God was not really with the Jewish people. It was decided to kindle the light and miraculously the oil lasted for the full eight days.

This is one of the miracles of Chanukah, and one of the reasons why the festival lasts eight days. It is also responsible for the creation of the Chanukah Menorah or *Chanukiah*, which, unlike the seven stick candelabra in the Holy Temple, would now have nine candles, one for each day of Chanukah and one for the *Shamash,* which was an extra candle utilized to light the other eight. The miracle is also proclaimed through a game, which is played especially by children during Chanukah. In Yiddish it is called "Dreidel" and In Hebrew it is "Siveevon". On the Dreidel which is a four-sided top are the four Hebrew letters which stand for the phrase, "A Great Miracle Happened There". The rules of the game give different results depending on which letter the Dreidel lands.

Once again there is a connection in these traditions to the B'nei Anusim. Like the *Chanukiah*, the flame of the crypto-Jews will never be extinguished. Their passionate flame of survival, hope, dedication and courage is apparent as they make the return to their Jewish roots.

The Return of Rachel Loya

On the day that the Israeli television crew arrived, I was bringing together a *Bet Din*, a religious court, to conduct the return, the conversion of Rachel Loya. Rachel is the daughter of Sonya Loya, the director of the Bat Tziyon Learning Center in Ruidoso, New Mexico.

Sonya, a crypto-Jew herself had done her return with me two years previously and devotes her life to the cause of the B'nei Anusim. Rachel was only twenty-one years old and had studied with me of her own volition for over a year. I taught her how to read Hebrew, the customs and ceremonies of the Jewish calendar, the life cycle of the Jew, the most important prayers of the synagogue, the content of the Jewish Bible, and Jewish history. Now it was time to culminate Rachel's year of study and commitment through the Conversion (*Geirut*) and Return ceremony.

The reporter for Israel television covered the conversion ceremony. The *Bet Din,* which was made up of myself, Cantor Marc Phillipe, and Mr. Harold Peitzer who is the *Gabbai,* or sexton of my synagogue and attends services every single day. The *Bet Din* asked Rachel several questions about Judaism, about her reasons for wanting to convert, about her religious beliefs, and how she intended to live her life as a Jew.

In addition to Rachel, her mother and father, and grandparents were in attendance. Once the *Bet Din* was satisfied that Rachel was adequately conversant with the principles and teachings of Judaism, she was guided into the second room where the actual Mikvah, or Ritual Bath is located. The female witness to Rachel's immersion was Sharon Cosby who had also returned to Judaism a year before. Rachel took a full shower and then went into the Mikvah. When she was ready, Sharon called the *Bet Din.* Although we were outside, we could hear the splashes of the three immersions and hear her recite the two blessings.

I asked Sharon to watch as Rachel recited the words in Hebrew, *Baruch Atah Adonye Eloheinu Melech Ha-*

Olam Asher Kidshanu BiMitzvotav Vitzivanu Ahl Ha-Tiveelah, "Blessed are You, O Lord, our God, Who has Sanctified us by His Commandments and Has Commanded us regarding Immersion." Rachel then completely immersed herself in the sacred waters of our Mikvah. Assuming the fetal position Rachel did not hold onto the walls of the bath. The position of Rachel reflected the idea that she was emerging from the womb of her "mother", in this case, Judaism, as her soul was symbolically being "reborn" as a Jew.

113

Rachel then recited the second blessing, "*Baruch Atah Adonye Eloheinu Melech HaOlam Sheh-heh-Cheyanu, ViKeeyimanu, ViHiggeeyanu, Lazman Hazeh*", "Blessed are You, O Lord, Ruler of the Universe, Who Has Kept us in life, Who has Sustained us, and Who has Enabled us to Reach this Day."

We heard the words of Rachel's prayer and Sharon watched the immersion. Rachel completely immersed herself a third time in the holy waters of the Mikvah without any recitation of words. After each correct immersion, Sharon declared, "Kosher" which means "Acceptable according to Jewish practice." The members of the Bet Din returned to the room where the questioning had taken place and waited for Rachel.

When she returned a short time later, she read the prayer, "*Sh'ma Yisrael*" in Hebrew. The "*Sh'ma*" which is found in the Torah, in the Book of Deuteronomy (6: 4-9 is the most important affirmation of the Jewish religion. We are commanded to recite the *Sh'ma* twice every single day we live, once in the evening and once in the morning. The *Sh'ma* is found in our liturgy and is part of our daily

Ma'ariv, or evening service, as well as part of our Shacharit, or morning service. In addition it is also recited before we go to sleep at night. If a Jewish man or woman knows that he or she is about to die, the *Sh'ma* is the last prayer that is said before one passes away.

The English translation of the words of the *Sh'ma* are as follows:

"Hear, O Israel, the Lord our God, the Lord is One. And you shall love the Lord your God with all your heart, with all your soul, and with all your might. And these words which I command you this day, shall be in your heart. And you shall teach them diligently to your children. And you shall speak of them when you sit in your house, and when you walk by the way, when you lie down and when you rise up. And you shall bind them as a sign upon your hand and they shall be as frontlets between your eyes, and you shall write them upon the doorposts of your house and upon your gates."

After reading the *Sh'ma* fluently in Hebrew, Rachel then read a "Declaration of Faith" in which she fully accepted Judaism as her way of life and agreed to raise any children with which she might be blessed in the Jewish way. I then read aloud in Hebrew and English the *Teudat Geirut*, "The Certificate of Conversion" which was signed and witnessed by the three members of the Bet Din. I conferred upon Rachel her new Hebrew name, *Racheil bat Avraham V'Sarah*, Rachel the Daughter of Abraham and Sarah.

The Israeli television crew videoed the conversion and interviewed Rachel and many of those who were present. Rachel and her mother were emotional about her return, and this ceremony was an example of the B'nei Anusim returning to Judaism generation by generation.

That same afternoon, the Israeli television crew was able to film the wedding ceremony of John Garcia and Elaine Tremblay. John is one of the B'nei Anusim who did his formal return years ago, and Elaine, who had also converted with me. They met at the synagogue, fell in love, and chose to be married during the festival of Chanukah.

Chanukah serves as a reminder of defiance to both the Syrian-Greek Hellenists and the Spanish Inquisitors that, not only did our ancestors survive, but that they have continued to practice the Jewish traditions of the centuries that have sustained us as a people from ancient times to the present day. John Garcia has not only returned to his Jewish roots, but he reads Torah for our congregation regularly, is capable of leading services, has had an Adult Bar Mitzvah, lives a life of a religious Jew, and continues to study Judaism.

The Israeli television reporter interviewed John and Elaine, and John spoke passionately about his crypto-Jewish background and how proud he was of his Jewish identity. The wedding ceremony was very traditional. Prior to the wedding taking place two observant Jews signed as witnesses to the Ketubah, the Jewish Wedding Document, which is written in Aramaic. John performed the obligation of *Badecken* in which he place the veil over his bride's face. At the beginning of the ceremony Elaine encircled the groom seven times.

As the officiating Rabbi, I chanted the *Birkat Eirusin*, the blessings for the Betrothal ceremony, which is said over a cup of Kosher wine. The groom and bride each took a sip of wine. Then came the ring ceremony. John took the ring and facing Elaine, placed it upon her right forefinger. Tradition says that the right forefinger is used for two reasons. First because that finger is easiest for the two witnesses to clearly see, and secondly, because the vein from that finger leads to the most direct route to the heart. As John placed the ring, he said to Elaine, "*Haray aht Mikudeshet Lee B"tabaat Zo, K'dat Moshe V'Yisrael*", "By this ring you are consecrated to me as my wife according to the law of Moses, and the people of Israel".

In our synagogue we have a double ring ceremony and Elaine placed the second ring on John's right forefinger and said these words from The Song of Songs, one of the five scrolls in the Jewish Bible, which I call "The Love song of the Jewish Bible." After the ring ceremony, I read from the Ketubah which was signed prior to the ceremony beginning.

After the reading of the Ketubah, Cantor Marc Philippe chanted the Sheva Brachot, the "Seven Blessings" over the second cup of wine. The seven blessings reflect the good wishes and prayers of all those in attendance, family and friends, who are wishing the couple all good things, happiness, health, children, peace and prosperity. John and Elaine once again each took a sip from the cup of wine.

Wine in Judaism is a symbol of sanctity and joy. Cantor Marc Philippe then sang the song "Jerusalem of Gold" for the couple. We then placed a Tallit, or Prayer Shawl, over them. This is a Sephardic custom which is indicative of God enveloping the couple with Divine blessings.

When a person puts on a Tallit, the following words are said, *Baruch Atah Adonye Eloheinu Melech HaOlam Asher Kidshanu B"Mitzvotav ViTzeevanu LiHeetateif Ba TzeeTzeet*, "Blessed are You O Lord our God Who Has Sanctified us by His Commandments and Has commanded us to envelop ourselves with the Fringes."

As the couple felt the spirituality of the tallit around them I offered the Priestly Benediction over them, as the Cantor and I place our hands over them. The translation of those Hebrew words are as follows: "May the Lord bless you and keep you, May God's face shine upon you and be gracious unto you, May God's face turn to you and grant you Shalom."

Following that blessing, I placed a glass wrapped in a napkin by John's foot and explained that the glass symbolizes that at a wedding our full glass of wine has also a drop of sorrow to remember some of the saddest times in the history of the Jewish people including the destruction of the two Holy Temples, the expulsion of the Jews during the Spanish Inquisition, and the six million Jews who perished during the Holocaust. The causes of those tragedies were hatred, racism, and bigotry. By destroying or breaking the glass we symbolically eliminate those evil forces and the only sentiments that remains are love, compassion and understanding, which are the spiritual pillars of a loving marriage.

As John broke the glass and kissed the bride, we all sang "*Siman Tov* and *Mazal Tov*" which means it is a good sign and good luck! I offered the prayer over the Challah, giving a piece of that special bread to the bride and groom, as we spent the rest of the time listening,

singing, and dancing to a wonderful band which played
happy Jewish music.

I felt truly content that the Israeli television crew had
presented and recorded a day that not only commemo-
rated the holiday of Dedication, Chanukah, but celebrat-
ed the full experience of the actual return of the B'nei
Anusim and the future of the crypto-Jews through the
beautiful and sacred ceremony of marriage.

118

Part Four

Reclaiming a Future from the Past

Chapter Ten

Suing the Catholic Church

T HE IDEA OF SUING THE CATHOLIC CHURCH HAS been on my mind for some time. I feel that the crimes against humanity, specifically killing Jewish and crypto-Jewish victims, has never been adequately addressed. Their communities were destroyed, and their properties were confiscated during that horrific time in world history. The Church has not expressed accountability comparable to the heinous nature of their actions.

Although Christianity holds itself up to be a religion that takes confession and atonement to be serious principles, I would like to see it act on those ideals in relation to the evil it inflicted upon the Jewish and crypto-Jewish people in the fifteenth and sixteenth centuries. Painful torture devices were used by the Church on the victims of the Inquisition, when their only crime was to remain loyal to Judaism and refuse to embrace Jesus as their God! Condemning crypto-Jews to be burned at the stake, if they were not sincere in their conversion to Christianity, was a horrible crime by the Church and its accomplice the Spanish Crown that has slipped unnoticed into the shroud of history.

These conversions, forced by the threat of death, are remembered in the Hebrew term anusim, which as I stated earlier, literally means "victims of rape". These were people forced by spiritual rapists, in this case the religious leaders of the Catholic Church, to do that which was against their will. As a religious person, I cannot remain silent and allow them to escape admission of liability for the evil acts that they committed against Spanish Jews and crypto-Jews.

The subject of suing the Church seems to be the only viable avenue of appropriate action that will force the Catholic Church to recognize its accountability in these crimes against humanity. With this in mind, the theme of the Thirteenth Annual Anusim Conference held in El Paso on August 19-21, 2016, was "Potential Alternatives for a Lawsuit against the Inquisition".

I invited an attorney from New York, Jay Sanchez, to be our keynote speaker on this controversial subject. Sanchez, who was raised as a Catholic and learned of his Jewish roots several years ago, told me that he had read an article in the *New York Times* about a previous Anusim Conference in which the question of suing the Church had been addressed. He had been in contact with Sonya Loya, and her affirmative response and passion on the subject had inspired him to do research on the legal aspects of this potential lawsuit.

As a result, attorney Sanchez was invited to Israel where he presented a lecture on this subject at a conference held at the Netanya Academic College in Netanya. After seeing a talk on this subject by Sanchez on YouTube, I decided to call him. After several interesting phone conversations, I invited him to be the keynote speaker at the thirteenth annual conference.

On the evening prior to the Conference, we convened a meeting of ten prominent El Paso attorneys, along with

Sonya Loya and board members of the Anusim Center of El Paso with the goal of learning from them their perspective on the feasibility of pursuing such a lawsuit. After hearing Jay Sanchez' presentation, each lawyer was given the opportunity to offer his perspective on the topic at hand. Only two of the attorneys, namely John and Ralph Garcia, had any substantive knowledge of the crypto-Jewish phenomenon. The discussion lasted for over an hour, and the conclusions of the attorneys present were both helpful and objective, but they had concerns about the feasibility of the successful conclusion of such a lawsuit.

123

Their first concern was about financial expenses, including the long time frame required to prepare the legal documentation. They saw the need to apply for grants to support the project and the need for bringing aboard academic experts, historians, and volunteers before such a court case could even be considered. I could understand their points of view, but I also felt that their approach would all but guarantee that no such proceedings would be realistic ever. A few of the attorneys were so skeptical in their remarks that they expressed the opinion that there were too many obstacles to even consider such a lawsuit. These concerns included the problem of the statute of limitations, determining the appropriate location for such hearings, addressing the correct defendant in the suit namely the government of Spain or the Catholic Church.

Although I understood the concerns of these dedicated attorneys, I felt that their reluctance to pursue this legal case would only allow the Church to once again hide its accountability and to deny its culpability for its dreadful crimes against my ancestors! Even though such a lawsuit might have flaws and would require extensive preparation, I believe that litigating against the Catholic Church would raise the issue for public, open discussion and would expose the plight of crypto-Jews to international discussion.

An additional concern of Sonya Loya, Jay Sanchez and others is the fear that there could be some severe repercussions from the clergy, the hierarchy, and the members of the Catholic Church toward individuals and groups who pursued these legal actions against the Church. Perhaps, a display of overt anti-Semitism toward the plaintiffs in the suit or even counter legal actions from the defendants might be the result of such legal accusations. In spite of these fears, I believe that the time is right and that the action is long overdue. One of the main reasons for this is that the present Pontiff of the Catholic Church, Pope Francis, is a man who has shown compassion, a thirst for justice and has displayed a welcoming relationship with the Jewish community.

When I visited Buenos Aires a few years ago, I had the privilege to see a unique display in the Buenos Aires Metropolitan Cathedral of a mural commemorating the victims of the Shoah. And while this display was inaugurated by Cardinal Antonio Querrachio, it was Pope Francis, then Cardinal Jorge Bergoglio, who expanded the memorial to include the victims of those Jewish Argentinians who were murdered in the terrorists attacks in the Israeli Embassy and AMIA, the Jewish Community Center. This display is extremely important because it is one of the only Cathedrals in the world in which a Jewish memorial is present.

In addition to the mural, a Tree of Life, a Menorah, the Tablets of the Law, and the Star of David are engraved on the frame. As Cardinal, Bergoglio made sure that his auxiliary bishops attended the annual commemoration of these terrorist attacks. In 2010 when he attended himself, he declared that the attack was "another link in the chain of sorrow and persecution that the chose people of God has suffered in history". He also hosted the annual day of remembrance for Kristallnacht at the Cathedral.

As Pope Francis, he has prayed at the Western Wall. In a meeting of Jewish leaders at the Vatican in 2013 he stated that, "Because of our common roots, a true Christian cannot be anti-Semitic." When the Pope visited Juarez, Mexico in February 2016, I suggested to a reporter from the *El Paso Times* that it would be appropriate for the Pope to visit with a group of crypto-Jews who live in El Paso and Juarez, but it did not happen. I believe this is the appropriate time for such a discussion to take place. In addition to the possibility that Pope Francis might be receptive to a dialogue about the Church's need to address its guilt for the crimes against the Jewish people during the Inquisition, there is another reason why I feel that such a discussion needs to occur now.

Today, there are several groups providing important information about the anusim, the crypto-Jews, and the conversos. The Institute for Sefardi and Anousim Studies at the Netanya Academic College, the Society for Crypto-Judaic Studies, the Center for Latino-Jewish Relations at Texas A&M Campus, and the Anusim Center of El Paso are among the organizations and cultural centers that can provide the resources necessary to disseminate important information on this subject. The result of such a conversation would lead to public awareness, dialogue, and exchange of ideas, which would spread to the unknown number of people who have crypto-Jewish roots in the world today. The continued discussion on this controversial subject is well worth it. Only time will tell if this lawsuit and this conversation will take place!

Epilogue

The Third Commandment
and the Hidden Guilt of the Church

THE THIRD COMMANDMENT REMINDS US THAT
God speaks to each of us. God speaks to us in
many ways, sometimes in whispers, sometimes
in dreams, sometimes in visions, sometimes in the synagogue or church or mosque, sometimes in our homes,
sometimes at the bedside of a loved one in a hospital,
sometimes by the crib of a newborn child, sometimes at
times of distress, sometimes at happy occasions, sometimes through miracles, sometimes in our average daily
lives.

I believe that we are living at a time when we need to
hear the voice of God, no matter how that divine message comes to us. Ever since my beloved father, Cantor
David Leon, was summoned to God several years ago, I
have also heard God's message through my father's voice.
I now also hear God's voice through the souls of the hundreds of thousands of my ancestors, some of whom who
were tortured in God's name, some of whom were burned
alive at the stake, some of who were forcibly converted,
some of whom were expelled from Spain and Portugal.
God is trying to speak to us today. I mentioned in a previous chapter that God spoke to me that the divine promise that the Jewish people would be as numerous as the

"sands of the sea and the stars in the sky" would be fulfilled when the descendants of the B'nei Anusim return to their precious heritage.

It is my hope and my prayer that those who read this book, whatever their religion, ethnicity, race or nationality will be motivated to bring the story of the crypto-Jews and B'nei Anusim to the world. I believe that if we can work together to teach their message, then we will make the world better and perhaps be prepared for redemption and peace. If the leaders of the Church would take responsibility for their heinous acts against the Jewish people during the Inquisition and then offer a hand of atonement, love, and unity to the Jewish people, they would help to pave that road of deliverance.

If the Jewish people would heed the voice of God and welcome the people of anusim background, who wish to return to their Jewish roots, whether in Israel or the Diaspora, and express forgiveness and unity with our Christian neighbors, then perhaps God's promise of a true Messianic age would be realized. If our Muslim brothers and sisters would insist that the peaceful teachings of Islam prevail over those who have done violence in its name, then together, Christians, Muslims and Jews could become one in our universal goal of creating a world of justice, compassion and peace.

If people of all faiths would grasp the outstretched hands of the victims of a previous age of brutality, which had been committed in a misguided interpretation of God's command and would instead embrace all children of God who have suffered and continue to suffer today, then we together could bring harmony to the world.

The history of the B'nei Anusim could help the entire world to recognize the violence of past and the atrocious acts that are being done in God's name today. Knowing that history could inspire people of all faiths to be united against the use of violence for religious purposes and respond to God's voice and bring Shalom, fulfillment, and redemption to the entire world.

AMEN

Appendix

My Father Speaks to Me from Above:
Shalom is on its Way

MY FATHER CANTOR DAVID J. LEON WAS called to the Almighty on Rosh Hashanah in the year 2002. From that moment on, as I consider the significance of the Lord calling him on that holy day on the Jewish calendar, and even now as I write these words, my father continues to talk to me.

Throughout his life my dad touched thousands of people. He was a very spiritual man. He was a Cantor, a Hazzan. He was an incredible teacher. He brought hundreds of Jewish children into the Covenant of Abraham, through the ritual of Brit Milah. He trained so many students for their Bar or Bat Mitzvah. He officiated at marriages and funerals. He was very wise and perceptive and counseled many people. He was never afraid to speak his mind. He was the ideal *Shaliach Tzibor*, the person given the awesome responsibility to represent the entire community during prayer services. When he passed on, I received a multitude of letters, notes, and phone calls from rabbis, cantors, and his former students who credited him with inspiring them throughout their lives. On his tombstone I wrote, "Our Sweet Singer of Israel". When God called David Leon to heaven that day of the Jewish New Year, I knew in my heart, that I would hear his sweet voice again. This book is both a tribute to him and a message to the world that he wants to me to deliver.

When I say that my father speaks to me, let me try to explain. I don't know. I cannot say that my father talks to me in the same voice, in the same manner, that he did when he was alive, or even in a way that I can illustrate in normal everyday terms. To describe the way that he communicates with me is similar to trying to understand what the Torah means when it says that "God spoke to Moses". Did Biblical conversations with the Almighty take place in the same way that I would talk to my neighbor today? The answer is once again, "I don't know!"

My grandson was watching the movie "The Ten Commandments" and asked me if the voice from the burning bush was really the voice of God. In that circumstance, I could easily say that it was not God's voice, but the voice of an actor in the film. I cannot imagine how the Lord did speak to Moses from the bush. The best way I can express how my father communicates with me is through thoughts that enter my mind, an occasional touch on my arm or back, and sometimes I do believe that I actually hear his voice.

Another method of receiving messages from him is that events happen to me that are coincidental and unpredictable that give me guidance, inspiration, or protection from danger that I never saw coming. I believe that these occurrences are also the result of my father's intervening in my life. I know that this sounds supernatural or unbelievable, and that you might think that I am either hallucinating or that I am outright, "out of my mind". Believe me I myself have entertained these thoughts. I have shared these experiences with some family and close friends, and occasionally even from the pulpit.

As a person whose religion believes in angels, I might even attribute these unusual experiences to the possibility that my father is now a kind of "guardian angel" for me. I have read many books over the years, such as *Beyond the Light* and *Heaven is For Real,* that describe the experiences of people who momentarily have left this world, went to heaven or the world beyond this world. This is not the case of my adventure with my father's communicating with me. I have not died. I have not gone to heaven, and I am not entirely sure where my father's soul is, since he never told me. But, I feel with all my being, from the deepest depths of my heart, that David Leon speaks to me and guides me, and now he wants me to share these thoughts with you. I am passionate about sharing with you his message to the world.

133

A World of Peace

From my earliest recollections of my father while he was alive, I was aware that so much of his life was devoted to doing things such as teaching lessons, singing prayers, organizing meetings, and visiting people, all done to help bring peace into the world. The horrific attack on New York which occurred on 9/11/2001 had a profound effect on him. He was aware that his granddaughter Shoshana, my oldest child, was actually at the restaurant "Windows of the World" the night before the tragedy, but for the "grace of God", she could have easily been taken from us on that infamous day. This violent act of terrorism woke many of us up to the enormity of evil that exists in the hearts of some people that they would murder thousands of innocent human beings without remorse or feeling.

The rest of that year my father and I had numerous discussions about this subject, and I could see tears in his eyes when he thought about it too much. My dad was always such an optimistic person when it came to encouraging others, when he visited people who were suffering, and when he talked to children or led a service, but somehow part of him never recovered from that tragic day.

134

I remember calling him and telling him that we canceled Hebrew school that day because we had received an alert that this terrorist action might be aimed at Jewish institutions in other parts of the United States. It saddened him. The following day we held a special service in our sanctuary simply to pray for Shalom, and my dad at the age of eighty-six participated in that worship and led the singing of the Hebrew blessing, *Oseh Shalom Bimromav*, which asks God who provides peace unto the heavens to bring that peace upon all of us on earth. I felt my father's pain as he led that chant.

Every week I found David Leon expressing his concern about the peaceful future of the world. It was almost as if this man who had always given others hope at difficult times, needed reassurance himself that one day there would be world peace. Almost one year to the day of the tragedy, he was called to the Almighty on September 8th, 2002. Shortly thereafter, he began speaking to me from beyond the grave.

The first time I heard my father's voice was on the Friday night after his death. It happened to be a special

Sabbath on the Jewish calendar entitled, "*Shabbat Shuvah*", which means "The Sabbath of Return". It falls on the Saturday between the Jewish High Holy Days of Rosh Hashanah and Yom Kippur. The theme of that service is connected to "repentance and return". As we began the service, I sang a traditional Shabbat song entitled "*Shalom Aleichem*" which means "Peace Be unto You". As I was singing, I could actually hear my dad chant very loudly in my ear the Hebrew word, "*Shalom*" over and over again. Shalom means "peace" in English.

According to Jewish tradition two angels are assigned the task by God to visit every home in the Jewish community on Friday night and report to God what they have observed. If the "good" angel notices that the family is together, having observed the Shabbat with the lighting of candles, saying the prayer over the wine, eating the special bread called "Challah" and singing songs and acting in a loving way, the family is blessed and the "evil" angel must say, "Amen". However, if the "evil" angel sees a home where no traditions are observed, where there is pettiness, and bickering, the angel wishes bad thoughts upon that home, and the "good" angel must say," Amen." Perhaps, what I really heard that evening was the angel of my father singing in a spiritual voice, and I heard my father tell me that his desire was that I do everything in my power to bring true "Shalom" to my entire congregation and to every person that I see. The world is in such need of Shalom, that I must reach out and carry that message to people of all faiths.

Peace is the blessing which is more important than anything else. With so many leaders of nations and religions preaching hatred and evil, my father wanted to assure me, especially on Shabbat, the day God rested after creating humanity, that what God wants is in this beautiful world that He created for you and me is for mankind to stop doing evil in His name, and instead to bring peace and harmony to the world. That Friday evening I truly felt the presence of my father through the *Shalom Aleichem* prayer and through the new interpretation that he communicated to me. We have every opportunity to devote our lives to this concept of world peace and few of us even bother.

136

As many of us are aware today, the goal of the God that we believe in is to create a world of peace for all of humanity. The prophets spoke of this through their words and prophecies. Although there are differences among the monotheistic religions in traditions, customs, liturgy, and other practices, one common goal should unite us if we worship the same God, and that is to bring true peace to all of mankind. The message that I receive frequently from my father is that PEACE is still the main agenda in God's divine plan.

Unfortunately, since that tragic day on September 11, 2001, it has been apparent that some religious leaders are preaching a different message and attributing it to God. My father has told me that more than anything else, this really angers the Lord. He never told me how he knows that God is angered by the evil that "religious" people have done and are still doing, but nevertheless I believe my father's message.

What I understood my father to tell me as he was urging me to pursue the path of peace for the entire community, was that clergy who teach their adherents that God wants them to blow themselves up along with other innocent people, are in violation of this commandment. God is angry with those acts, and He will not forgive them.

Many are afraid to speak out against suicide bombings or honor killings which are promoted in the name of God or Allah, but my father is not and he wants all religious leaders to know that God is truly angered by their behavior and that God will ensure that they will be duly punished for violating the Third commandment. To God, it doesn't matter which religion one is representing, if violent actions are taken in God's name, it is abhorrent to the Lord, who gave us these commandments.

My father always loved to sing, or teach the Junior Choir to sing the final paragraph of the morning services. The paragraph begins with these words in Hebrew, *Sim Shalom Ba'Olam, Tova Uvracha Chein VaChesed V'Rachamim, Aleinu V'oll Kol Yisrael Amecha.* The translation is "Grant peace in the world, grace, mercy and kindness, upon us and upon all of Israel, Your nation."

In other words it is a request to God to envelop the world and the people of Israel with a lasting peace together with compassion, kindness, and mercy. There are several melodies which have been written for this liturgical piece, and my dad also composed two additional versions. Every time he chanted the prayer, or whenever he would lead the choir to sing it, he would offer a different melody. In his eyes the content of the "*Sim Shalom*" was worthy of the full attention of the worshipers. Since it always came toward the conclusion of the service when some attendees might not be entirely focused on this prayer after a long service, my father would revive their interest and participation by changing the melody periodically and offering the chant with a special spiritual interpretation.

He recently told me that the words of this prayer can open the windows of heaven, and God will also join the chorus! I suppose that this particular message from my father is a further indication that God truly pays attention especially when His worshipers are praying for peace with sincerity, devotion, and both musical and spiritual harmony.

Over the centuries since man first inhabited this earth, it should be clear that of all of the desires of our God of Justice, the most important is that humanity should be creating a world of peace. Sometimes each of us needs a wakeup call to get us back on that proper path to peace. It is my sincere hope, and that of my father, that all of God's creatures of all colors, religions, and ethnicities will soon put aside that which divides us and instead will come together with a common goal of unity in spreading the message of Shalom throughout the world.

138

Some Related Gaon Books Publications

Historical Fiction on B'nei Anusim Life

Mario Martinez
2009. *Converso.*
2016. *Abran and Isabel's Hidden Faith*

Isabelle Medina Sandoval
2009. *Guardians of Hidden Traditions*
2012. *Hidden Shabbat*

Angelina Muñiz-Huberman.
2014. *Dreaming of Safed.*

Sandra K. Toro
2010. *By Fire Possessed.* Out of print.
2011. *Princes, Popes and Pirates.* Out of print.
2012. *Secrets Behind Adobe Walls.*
2016. *Beacon of Hope: Doña Gracia Nasi*

Non-fiction Titles on Sephardic Life

Silvia Hamui Sutton.
　　　2017. *Lyrical Eroticism in Judeo-Spanish Songs.*
　　　2009. *Cantos judeo-españoles: simbología, poética y
　　　　　visíon del mundo.*
Nina B. Lichtenstein. 2017. *Sephardic Women's Voices: Out of North Africa.*
Orit Rabkin. Forthcoming. *Emma Lazarus: Sephardic Woman of Letters.*
Ron D. Hart. 2016. *Sephardic Jews: History, Religion and People.*
William Samelson. 2014. *Sephardic Legacy: Songs and Stories from Jewish Spain.*
Susana Weich-Shahak. 2014. *Moroccan Sephardic Romancero.*

Gaon Books

publishes books on Jewish life
with a focus on Sephardic traditions.

It is associated with the non-profit
Gaon Institute for Tolerance Studies
a 501-c-3 organization and sponsor of the

GaonWeb

includes Gaon Books, GaonWeb Films
and conferences on Jewish learning.

For more information go to:
www.gaonweb.org